CITIZENS RISING

FOUNDER OF INTERNEWS
DAVID HOFFMAN

FiNGERPRINT!

Published by

FiNGERPRINT!

An imprint of Prakash Books India Pvt. Ltd.

113/A, Darya Ganj, New Delhi-110 002,
Tel: (011) 2324 7062 – 65, Fax: (011) 2324 6975
Email: info@prakashbooks.com/sales@prakashbooks.com

facebook www.facebook.com/fingerprintpublishing
twitter www.twitter.com/FingerprintP, www.fingerprintpublishing.com
For manuscript submissions, e-mail: fingerprintsubmissions@gmail.com

ISBN: 978 81 7234 541 9

Processed & printed in India

PRAISE FOR *CITIZENS RISING*

"No one is better equipped than David Hoffman to analyze and explain the transformative shift in the role of the media in the world today. With grace and clarity, he helps us all to understand better how the media shapes our politics, economics, culture, and history."
—Lee H. Hamilton, former Congressman, Director of the Center on Congress, Indiana University

"For more than thirty years David Hoffman has been at the center of a global community of media activists who have transformed politics, diplomacy and development. This book could not be more timely as citizens, newly empowered by digital technologies, are challenging the old order in every corner of the world. The book brings to life the events behind the headlines of recent history and demonstrates the power of media at the forefront of political change."
—Kathy Calvin, President and CEO, the UN Foundation

"Many books have been written about the power of technology in global politics. But ultimately social and political change is about how technology is used by people to tell stories, report previously unknown facts, and spread information to mass audiences. David Hoffman, who has been at the center of the media development field for the past thirty years, tells the stories of people from Russia to Afghanistan to Tunisia to Burma who built the media that transformed their societies—and hence the world. A must read for anyone interested in understanding the power of media and the Internet in political transformations."

—Rebecca MacKinnon, Author of *Consent of the Networked*

"The power of the media to change the world and promote democracy is still all powerful—just ask David Hoffman, who has written the most optimistic and well argued book on the new media in decades."

—Ahmed Rashid, Author of *Taliban*

"David Hoffman eloquently explains why media is one of the most powerful—and most poorly understood—forces for social change. *Citizens Rising* is a critical guide to understanding the power of media for civil society and ways in which participatory media is redefining our political and civic landscape. Written by a man who's been one of the key actors in helping build free and open media around the world, *Citizens Rising* is informed by Hoffman's deep knowledge and practice."

—Ethan Zuckerman, Director, MIT Center for Civic Media and Author of *Rewire*

"With the fervor of someone whose life has been devoted to promoting a free press as an essential partner in a democracy, David Hoffman has written a stirring book. He shows how digital technology grants a voice to citizens, threatens the most brutal dictators, and, however unevenly, promises a better tomorrow."

—Ken Auletta, *The New Yorker*

This book is dedicated to the thousands of media activists
around the world who risk their lives to keep us free.

And to Jane, the light of my life.

CONTENTS

CONTENTS

INTRODUCTION

The shift from media controlled by a few to media owned by all of us portends a revolution as great as that which followed the invention of the printing press.

The dynamic growth of media and information is transforming every aspect of our social, economic, cultural and political lives. Eight hundred Arab language satellite channels, half a billion Chinese online, 150 percent mobile phone penetration in India—the ubiquity and plurality of media represents an unprecedented opportunity to reinvent development and governance. Today's media make it far more difficult to lead countries to war, and unacceptable to allow famine or the violent suppression of human rights. The voiceless are finding their voice. Information is power. We are in this together and we are all connected.

Citizens Rising: Independent Journalism and the Spread of Democracy portrays media's role in breaking the reign of ignorance and fear that are the first lines of defense for despots everywhere. (By "media" I refer to all means of the social distribution of information through technology, from radio to Twitter.) In the developed world, where we suffer a daily glut of information, we often take media for granted and don't fully appreciate why people would

11

stand in front of tanks and risk their lives for the right to speak. But large parts of the world live in information poverty that limits their ability to compete in the global economy and to participate in the most important decisions that affect them. Free and independent media are leveling this playing field and are empowering people with the information they need to take control of their lives.

Surprisingly, although media is one of the most powerful forces for social change the world has ever known, historians and policymakers largely fail to recognize the transformational way that media have been used by political actors as drivers, and not merely observers, of our recent history. Even Professor Joseph Nye of Harvard University, one of the most astute analysts of foreign policy, was late in recognizing the power of media in his many volumes on "soft power." And scholars like Amartya Sen, who won a Nobel Prize in economics and gained fame for his assertion "No substantial famine has ever occurred in any country with a relatively free press," have never fully examined the role of media in development. Yet media are essential to all aspects of development—from reducing corruption through transparency to building civil society and the rule of law. Indeed, the best measure of a country's freedom may well be the degree of the media's independence from the state, even more than the existence of periodic elections.

The so-called "Facebook Revolutions" and upheavals of the Arab Spring have finally changed much of this, awakening pundits and policymakers to the power of media in recent movements for social change. It is not the technology itself, however, that makes history: people do. The cyber activists who toppled dictatorships in the Middle East are but the latest in a succession of media visionaries who have altered the course of history. *Citizens Rising* is the untold story of some of these remarkable leaders who turned new communications technologies into weapons of revolutionary change. Ironically, before the uprisings in the Middle East, the world's press reported on few of these stories, yet the accounts reveal significant forces that have shifted—and continue to shift—the balance of power in some of the most important historical events of our lifetimes.

Open information is both the means and a fulfillment of human freedom. It is through the curtailment of information that our liberties are denied and it is through the access and expression of information that we set ourselves free. From Watergate to the Arab Spring, journalists and media activists have challenged the abuse of power. Whether in a democracy or a closed society, people power is exercised to one degree or another through the media. As the globalization of finance and culture makes the world ever more interdependent, the spread of new technologies and the democratization of the mass media pose an existential challenge to any authoritarian regime.

If the twentieth century will be remembered as the most violent in human history, the next century holds the promise of something different—an unprecedented expansion of human freedom. Arguably, war has been the organizing principle of the last hundred years; information will be seen as the organizing principle of the twentyfirst century. War defined our borders, propelled our economies, drove our scientific and technological development, supported our ideologies, and shaped our cultural attitudes about race and gender. But today, war is becoming less frequent and less effective. The physical borders that our armies were built to defend are less salient to our security. Ballistic missiles, air transport, satellites and information technologies transcend national borders, as the attacks of 9/11 so tragically proved. It is revealing that the fastest growing segment of our national defense is cyber security.

With advances in digital communications and information technologies and the spread of mobile phones, we are entering the dawn of the third great wave of egalitarianism. Like its predecessors, democracy and socialism, the Information Revolution will be the primary force for change for decades to come. It has already altered the course of history, overturned dictatorships, accelerated globalization, and given voice to the poorest of the poor. Like the democratic revolutions of the eighteenth century, the information revolution recognizes our rights as equal members of civil society to access news and information about the world we live in, to express ourselves without fear or censorship, to freely assemble, and to participate in governing our communities. Like the socialist revolutions of the nineteenth and early twentieth centuries that sought economic justice through the equal distribution of social wealth, this revolution aspires to share the totality of humanity's information capital. Information wealth is not a zero-sum game. The enrichment of others makes us all wealthier, while the hoarding of information circumscribes our inalienable right to share in human knowledge. The Information Revolution fulfills the promise of democracy that all are created equal, and the aspiration of socialism—from each according to their abilities, to each according to their needs.

Today the news is no longer a spectator sport; the media are all of us. The stories described in the pages to follow are examples of what the physicist and author Dr. Robert Fuller calls "psychotectonic shifts," those seminal moments when an established social and psychological framework crumbles and a new moral reality takes its place. With the democratization of information, such shifts occur more often and spread more rapidly than ever before. Freedom begins with an awakening in human consciousness. Today, as the new media gives power to the rest of us, we are poised as never before to shape our own destiny.

Citizens Rising is divided into three parts. The first traces the evolution of media and their growing role at the center of civil society. Advances in technology have enabled new forces for social change to emerge that challenge the old political order. The introduction of satellite television at the height of the Cold War, for example, enabled Soviet and American audiences to overcome the geographic and ideological boundaries that separated them. In Afghanistan, the development of electronic media is transforming a tribal society into a modern democracy in the midst of war. Independent television played a role in bringing down General Musharraf's government in Pakistan and Eduard Shevardnadze's in Georgia and toppled other authoritarian regimes in "Color Revolutions" in Ukraine and Kyrgyzstan. Media are also at the forefront of the dramatic reforms that are democratizing Myanmar after decades of a repressive military dictatorship.

Technology alone, however, does not of itself lead to freedom. The second section of *Citizens Rising* looks at how some leaders have used (or abused) the power of the media. An examination of the former Yugoslavia and Rwanda reveals how media have been harnessed as instruments of war, ethnic cleansing, and genocide. But free and open media also have unparalleled powers for reconciliation and economic development, as is occurring in Kenya with the spread of inexpensive mobile telephony. Finally, the media's crucial role as a first responder in humanitarian emergencies became evident in the aftermath of the 2004 tsunami in Indonesia, as well as in Haiti following the earthquake of 2010.

The third part of the book considers how the ubiquity of the Internet and mobile phones is challenging authoritarian power today, from the Arab cyber activists who had prepared for years to launch the revolts of 2011 in Tunisia and Egypt to the activists operating in China's vast cyberspace, where an unprecedented online civil society has emerged. Finally, I will speculate on what it all might mean for offline freedoms and the future of the Internet.

A personal note: I became interested in the role of media and social change as a political activist, not as a journalist. Having participated in launching the anti-nuclear war movement in the US in the early 1980s, I was searching for a way to humanize the Soviet-American conflict and engage in a dialogue that could help de-escalate the arms race. The introduction of satellite television offered an opportunity to do just that, as I recount in the first chapter.

In the wake of the collapse of the Soviet Union and the occupied countries of Eastern Europe, thousands of independent television stations proliferated. Along with my colleagues Kim Spencer and Evelyn Messinger, I formed a nonprofit organization called Internews to support them. The media development field, as it came to be known, provided much-needed journalism training, technical support, and legal and regulatory advice. As other countries experience transitions to democracy and civil society, the need for media assistance continues to grow. Internews, one of the largest non-governmental media development organizations in the world, has worked in more than ninety nations and there are now more than one thousand other media development organizations around the globe.

My encounters with independent journalists, media entrepreneurs and activists have afforded me the privilege of getting to know some of the remarkable people who are described in the chapters that follow. These media visionaries are leaders of a democratic transformation of global politics and an information revolution that is reshaping our world faster than any previous force in human history. It is my hope that readers will come away from these pages inspired to make their own voices heard.

PART I

INDEPENDENT MEDIA
AND THE RISE OF
DEMOCRACY

WE DON'T HAVE SEX IN THE SOVIET UNION

As I walked along the polished floors and empty hallways of the Kremlin, I felt like a tightrope walker, out too far and too high. It was 1987, the apex of the Cold War, and I was deep inside the bowels of the enemy, carrying a letter that could potentially alter the course of history. I was acting as a citizen diplomat without portfolio, without anything official, except that piece of paper. I tapped my suit jacket to make sure it was still there, nestled in my inside pocket. This was a quixotic, some would say preposterous, initiative.

Seven years prior, in 1980, my partners Kim Spencer and Evelyn Messinger had produced the first live television broadcast using communications satellites in an experimental interactive program for PBS. Called *America at Thanksgiving*, the show was a technological feat back then, connecting six groups of Americans celebrating Thanksgiving across the country. It was an electrifying moment when two of the participants—a motorcycle gang member in Cambridge, Massachusetts and a cadet at a mess hall in Nellis Air Force base in Las Vegas— bypassed the moderator and began talking directly to one another. Evelyn turned to Kim and exclaimed, "Holy shit! Why can't we do this with the Russians?" Two years later Internews began producing a series of experimental "spacebridges," or *telemosts*, as they were called in Russian, linking astronauts and cosmonauts, scientists, veterans of World War II, and others. The exchanges gradually caught the attention of policy makers on both sides.

In February 1986, Soviet citizens eagerly awaited the coming Twenty-seventh Party Congress. There, the young and seemingly modern new general secretary, Mikhail Gorbachev, would present his plans for *perestroika*—the restructuring and reform of the sclerotic Soviet economic and political system. The dynamic young leader presented a stark contrast to the decrepitude of the three general secretaries who preceded him.

A few days before the Congress convened, the Politburo debated for two hours whether or not to broadcast "A Citizens' Summit," a spacebridge moderated by Phil Donahue in Seattle and Vladimir Pozner, a popular Russian television host, in Leningrad. Taped live and unedited, the interactive audience-to-audience format allowed Russian and American citizens to freely discuss topics that had been strictly taboo on Soviet television—everything from the gulags and the samizdat writings of Alexander Solzhenitsyn to sexual norms and the Beatles. This would be the first spacebridge to be broadcast widely in the United States; for the Soviets, such a dialogue would signal a dramatic break from the past. But the Soviet leadership was unable to arrive at a consensus.

The chairman of Soviet State Television and Radio, Alexander Aksyonov, later told me he made the decision to go ahead with the program on his own, and then went home that night and drank himself into a stupor, not sure whether he would have a job, or even his freedom, after the show aired. The next day, two hundred million Soviet citizens heard Phil

Donahue and his American audience question their Russian interlocutors about the lack of basic freedoms in the USSR. In one memorable moment a young woman in Leningrad answered Donahue's probing question about romantic relationships with Russian irony. "We don't have sex in the Soviet Union," she exclaimed. The program was so popular that Soviet State Television rebroadcast it three evenings in a row in prime time during the all-important Soviet Party Congress. This uncensored dialogue on television led ordinary Russians to believe that important social and political changes were in the making.

As the spacebridges attracted increasing attention in the US, Congressman George E. Brown Jr. from Riverside, California, agreed to introduce me to Tip O'Neill, the legendary speaker of the US House of Representatives. O'Neill was concerned about the growing threat of nuclear war and was eager to hear any ideas that might lessen the tension. When Congressman Brown and I sat down across a mahogany desk from the speaker, I laid out our proposal—to use satellite television to broadcast a live debate between the leaders of the US Congress and the Supreme Soviet. It would not be a negotiation; that was the province of the executive branch, not the parliament. Nor would it be anything official, although it would have the trappings of a diplomatic summit. Formally, it would only be a television show where individual legislators would express their personal opinions, not necessarily those of their governments. But it would look like the real thing, broadcast live from Capitol Hill and from the Kremlin, and it might just lead to a thaw in our frozen relationship.

With the prospect of such a high-visibility television dialogue, O'Neill saw an opportunity for Congress to insert itself into the most important and intractable foreign policy issue of the time. Soviet and American nuclear missiles were on hair-trigger alert. Arms control negotiations were going nowhere. Virtually all educational and scientific exchanges had been frozen. An enormous peace movement that rivaled the civil rights movement of the 1960s had elevated Soviet-American relations into the defining issue of the 1980s, putting pressure on policymakers to act. Still, we remained locked in our ritualized demonization, characterizing each other as the "evil empire" and "imperialist lackeys." It was time to break the ice and put a human face on the enemy. "What can I do to help?" O'Neill asked. I suggested he write a letter to his equivalent, the speaker of the Supreme Soviet. "Please draft it for me," he said.

It was thirty degrees below zero with a wind chill factor of minus-sixty when I arrived at Moscow's Hotel Rossiya just behind Red Square. Everyone in the city seemed to be surviving it in a fur hat but me. The hotel was an endless maze of totalitarian drabness punctuated with decorations of pure kitsch. After dialing an operator at the Kremlin and leaving a message that I was carrying a letter from Speaker O'Neill for Lev Tolkunov, the chairman of the Supreme Soviet, I waited several hours before the phone rang; an operator said a car would be there in ten minutes. Soon a black ZiL limousine appeared, and two minutes later we drove through the Spassky Gate into the Kremlin, where few Americans had ever ventured. Officers in heavy gray coats saluted. I happened to be in the middle of writing, in my spare time, a mystery novel that took place largely inside the Kremlin walls. I immediately realized that everything I had imagined was completely wrong. Where I had pictured tension, a sense of urgency, and the disorder of constant crises, there was in reality an almost antiseptic order amid the calm of bureaucratic paperwork. This did not feel like the command center of the evil empire; instead, it felt like ordinary people getting through their workday.

I entered the antechamber of Chairman Tolkunov's office, a cavernous room with twenty-foot-tall ceilings. On the far side was a map covering an entire wall, a bright red Soviet Union at its center. Gazing at it, with his back to me, hands clasped behind him in a Napoleonic pose, was the chairman's chief of staff. On the desk next to him were perhaps thirty separate phones, a measure of one's rank in the Soviet hierarchy. I took a seat and after a moment he turned and walked toward me. Although it was fairly dark inside, he was actually wearing sunglasses. I suppressed a laugh, but when he sat down, I reached into my jacket and put on a pair of my own, deliberately mimicking him. An awkward silence ensued and then we both broke up laughing. We would work closely together in the months ahead with an informality that was forged in this initial encounter.

He led me into the chairman's office. Huge picture windows framed the famed onion domes of Saint Basil's Cathedral. The chairman greeted me warmly and I explained to him what we had in mind, handing him Speaker O'Neill's letter. The necessity of strict parity was critical if we were to develop this potentially gamechanging project together. The Russians, it seemed to me, had an inferiority complex with regard to the West. It was, therefore, vitally important they be accorded equal status and respect from the beginning. Americans had always scoffed at the illegitimacy of the Soviet parliament; but by engaging with it on an equal basis, would we not, paradoxically, increase its power and independence?

Our proposal presumed that the speaker of the Soviet

parliament would jump at a chance to demonstrate symbolic parity with the American Congress. And, indeed, after Speaker Tikhonov read the translation, he smiled and said he was completely in favor of it. "Please draft a response," he said. Back at the hotel, I had to shake my head at the surreal absurdity of writing letters on behalf of the leaders of both the Soviet and American parliaments to each other.

A hundred fifty million people, the bulk of them in the USSR, watched each of the seven live broadcasts in the *Capital to Capital* series, as they were called, and the programs won several Emmy Awards. Peter Jennings, the longtime ABC News anchor, moderated each from the ornate House Ways and Means Committee Room on Capitol Hill in Washington. Leonid Zolotarevsky, a Russian newscaster, hosted from the Soviet parliament in the Kremlin. The symbolism was transformational. Instead of the usual acrimony that citizens in both countries were used to watching on television, they saw political leaders talking to each other thoughtfully and with respect. Subjects ranged from arms control and regional conflicts to human rights, the environment, and the fate of Jewish refuseniks.

No treaties were signed as a result, but the superpower conflict had changed from the scary—almost a half-century of an ever-escalating arms race—to something more human and subject to rational debate. Soviet viewers who were conditioned to perceive all American politicians as warmongers were stunned when an emotional Claude Pepper, the eighty-seven-year-old congressman from Florida, stood among his House colleagues, pounded his fist, and thundered, "I think the time has come for both of us to come under the scrutiny of common sense and get down to business about stopping the nuclear arms race and getting back to a sensible, friendly relationship. Is that possible?"

Satellite television literally breached the two countries' ideological and geographic borders, allowing viewers to eavesdrop on conversations between their political leaders. Throughout the 1980s, thanks to a dozen other live televised spacebridges, American and Russian citizens were able to meet each other, putting a human face on the "enemy" they had been taught to fear. As the *Capital to Capital* series came to a close in 1989, US-Soviet relations had changed in ways that were unimaginable at the start, with substantial arms reduction treaties signed and hundreds of thousands of citizen-to-citizen exchanges.

When the Berlin Wall fell and the Cold War came to an end, it was the power of information and the longing for freedom that won out. There were many factors that contributed to this, but among the most powerful and least understood were the media. "Why did the West win the Cold War?" asked Michael Nelson, a leading commentator at the time with the Reuters news agency. "Not by use of arms. Weapons did not breach the Iron Curtain. It was media that proved to be *mightier than the sword*."

In the Soviet Union, media opened a window to the West with its wealth and its freedoms, gave a voice to those silenced by censorship, and galvanized the people to act. It was media that breached the Iron Curtain with images of life in the West, which led the people living under Communism to realize they were falling behind the Free World. And it was media that spread news and information of protests and revolts from one corner of the empire to another and gave people a voice. Whatever pressures pushed Gorbachev to initiate political and economic reforms, it was through the media that the Soviet people experienced change.

Communication technologies have evolved dramatically in the following three decades, but media continues to be the most powerful force for social change the world has ever known. The Arab Spring that ignited in Tunisia in 2011 focused the world's attention on the techno-savvy cyber activists who deployed new digital media technologies to rally the masses against long-established dictatorships. These citizen journalists in the Middle East and elsewhere share a lineage with the citizen diplomats who helped bring an end to the Cold War. In both cases, technological innovation in the media—interactive satellite television in the 1980s and the Internet and social media today—produced a "psychotectonic shift" that vastly increased the power of social change activists. Both combined new technologies with "old" media in ways that dramatically shifted the existing political framework. *Capital to Capital* would not have been possible without establishment television—ABC News and Gosteleradio—just as YouTube citizen journalists now depend on Al Jazeera and CNN to amplify and enlarge their own audiences.

It is easy to make a fetish of technology, however; in the end, it is people who make the difference, individual innovators and activists who realize the colossal power of electronic media to bring about social change.

LIVE FROM MOSCOW :
THE BIRTH OF INDEPENDENT MEDIA

One of the most influential of a new generation of Soviet journalists was Eduard Sagalaev, the forty-year-old mustachioed head of Youth Programs at Soviet State Television. Like many of his compatriots, he came of age with a recognition that the USSR was falling behind the West. Born in Samarkand, half-Jewish and half-Uzbek, Sagalaev was something of an outsider in a Communist Party dominated by Russians. With strong ethnic features and a feline nervousness about him, he seemed oddly out of place on the twelfth floor of Ostankino, the Soviet State TV Center in Moscow. But as a former official on the Central Committee of the Communist Youth League, Sagalaev enjoyed the power of approving new television shows on his own authority.

Concerned that the West was increasingly seducing Soviet youth, higher Party officials urged him to do something to attract the next generation of Communists, something the bloated and bureaucratic state-run television was ill-equipped to do.

Imitating the live, interactive satellite television "spacebridge" format pioneered by his colleague Vladimir Pozner, Sagalaev launched an audacious new youth program called *12th Floor* in 1986. Producing live, interactive links with young people outside the studio, thereby avoiding the ubiquitous censors, *12th Floor* was an immediate sensation, as Ellen Mickiewicz recounts in *Changing Channels*, her definitive study of Russian television. With frank opinions, debate and even criticism of Party officials, *12th Floor* was by far the boldest political program yet to appear on Soviet television. It signaled the social changes about to convulse the nation. Such reforms on television prefaced the reforms that would transform the political space. Eduard Sagalaev, fully aware of the powerful role media would play in the coming alterations in the political landscape, commented presciently, "The process of creating new democratic organs of government power is beginning and, as never before, the greatest responsibility rests with the broadcast media."

Under withering criticism from Party hardliners, however, Sagalaev was forced to pull the plug on *12th Floor* in the fall of 1987. In compensation, he was promoted to head of television news. Before he left the Youth Programs Department, though, Sagalaev launched another show, a late-night news program he had been developing for several years. *Vzglyad*, or *Viewpoint*, became the single most popular program of the Gorbachev era.

Aiming to attract the nation's youth, Sagalaev wanted the *Vzglyad* presenters to look and sound more like their audience—young, modern, "thinking boys," rebels even, a Soviet version of the Beatles, he said. He recruited four young friends as hosts. They appeared on camera in sweatshirts. The broadcasts were live and uncensored with fast cutaways to rock music. Mickiewicz, described how "teenagers talked back from the safety of their stairwells and streets . . . the young people challenged officials; they told education officials that 'very little happens in school,' that 'they talk about duties, but you don't hear anything about rights.' They argued for the restoration of proscribed writers and wanted to know more about the West . . . and complained that their textbooks were woefully out of date. In every show, the plaint of the youth was repeated: 'Why are things decided on top and not here?'"

Despite its late-night time slot, *Vzglyad* quickly surpassed the ratings for *Vremya*, the main evening news show. If people couldn't vote in free elections, they could at least vote by what they watched. Television revealed a divide in Soviet society. On one hand, an older generation had grown numb in the monotony of Communist conformity, reflected in the boring evening newscasts on *Vremya*, where the same politicians were seen endlessly shaking hands or droning on in formulaic speeches; on the other hand, a younger generation, increasingly identified with Western styles, felt alienated when they were prevented from participating in the cultural revolution of the late sixties.

Soon other programs appeared in defiance of Soviet hardliners. Investigative journalism exposed the decay of the once-proud Soviet state; late night talk shows brought differing political viewpoints onto TV for the first time; Western music, which had been banned, filled the airwaves; and, as we shall see, coverage of the war in Afghanistan brought that conflict to the forefront of popular concerns.

Vzglyad was periodically taken off the air for one political transgression or another, sometimes for months at a time, but would then reappear. The political power of these media visionaries was evidenced in March 1989, however, in the first multi-candidate elections for the newly created Congress of People's Deputies, the supreme legislative body, when twelve television anchors won overwhelming victories, three of them *Vzglyad* presenters. Their election had the added benefit of securing them parliamentary immunity, protecting their speech on television. The young new voices in the media that Eduard Sagalaev had helped launch were gaining a constituency. They would continue to play significant roles in the post-Soviet media world as well.

Glasnost Unbound

When a government begins to lose control over its information space, its legitimacy is threatened. With fits and starts, Gorbachev's government loosened the tight control over the media that had suffocated Soviet life for seventy years. Although he trumpeted his new policy of *glasnost*, or "openness," it was only meant to be a tool for energizing the political and economic reforms of perestroika; but glasnost quickly took on a life of its own. One of the most significant examples was the establishment in 1989 of Interfax, the first independent news agency in the Soviet Union, created by officials from the International Service of Moscow Radio. Interfax routinely scooped the official news organs, bringing transparency to a country ruled by secrecy. The Communist Party maintained its control over the mass media, but in the tug of war between the reform faction and the hardliners, journalists began experimenting to test the boundaries of free speech.

Vladimir Starkov's weekly, *Agumentiy Facti,* was such a test. Started as an arcane paper for statisticians and economists with a circulation of around ten thousand, the publication under glasnost began describing the lives of ordinary people and reached sales of thirty-three million copies. For the first time,

Boris Pasternak's *Doctor Zhivago* appeared legally in 1986—
twenty years after the film version premiered in the West. In
addition, there were new movies, publications and TV shows
that made people shake their heads in disbelief that such
strident critiques could be happening in the heart of Soviet
Communism. In 1987, the publication of Anatoli Rybakov's
Children of the Arbat, the epic novel of life under Stalin, became
the publishing sensation of the perestroika era. *Repentance,*
Tengiz Abuladze's searing anti-Stalinist film, won the Grand
Jury Prize in Cannes the same year. Long suppressed, discussion
of the crimes of the Stalin period turned memory itself into a
political act. The trickle of uncensored media, begun with the
spacebridges and *12th Floor,* became a tidal wave the leadership
was unable to stop.

It would be wrong, however, to think that the masses were
all anti-Communists waiting for an outlet to air their grievances.
The population had grown up under Communism and largely
believed in its egalitarian ideology, if not its practice. Even a
liberal intellectual like TV host Vladimir Pozner marveled at
how his own thinking changed radically after Gorbachev's
ascendance "from a person who clung to the ideals of
socialism and Communism, who had refused to give up on his
convictions, who had refused to part with his illusions, and who
had attempted to preserve them by rationalizing the realities of
Soviet existence" to "wondering with a sense of repugnance
at how I had denied myself the most prized treasure a human
being is born with: open and independent thought." It was this
freedom to speak, he realized later, that "liberated" his mind
to think.

Perhaps the greatest shock for the Soviet people was the
media's coverage of the war in Afghanistan, which began on

Christmas Eve 1979 when Soviet troops invaded to prop up the increasingly isolated Communist government there. The war was taking a heavy toll—financially, militarily, and on the perception of Soviet military power abroad. The pressures on the draft army, which fell disproportionately on non-Russian conscripts of the USSR, accentuated the tensions already building in Russia's "autonomous" republics.

In 1987, when some relatively small independent television stations broadcast footage of caskets of Russian troops killed in Afghanistan being unloaded, there was an unspoken realization that the government could no longer count on its monopoly of the media to manage popular opinion. One of the gravest consequences of the war—even more than the strategic defeat it represented—was the realization that, in the aftermath of the withdrawal from Afghanistan, Russia would be unlikely to deploy its troops to intervene in Eastern Europe as it had done in the past, thus posing the real possibility of the breakup of its empire.

Satellites Break Out of Orbit

The reforms introduced by Mikhail Gorbachev in the Soviet Union emboldened people throughout the Communist Bloc in the East. As small demonstrations for freedom escalated into massive unrest, television played a central and ultimately decisive role in the East's liberation. The Soviet satellite countries grouped under the Warsaw Pact—including the German Democratic Republic, Czechoslovakia, Hungary, Poland, Romania, and the Baltic states of Estonia, Lithuania, and Latvia—were staggering under mounting debts to Western banks while their people became increasingly aware, to an extent greater even than the Russians, of how far they were slipping behind their West European neighbors. Television from Finland, West Germany, and Austria seeped across their borders, and home satellite dishes proliferated across Eastern Europe. Their demands for greater freedoms included one compelling argument that Russian citizens did not have—a desire to get rid of the humiliating foreign occupation and restore their national independence.

Television would play a central and decisive role in the liberation movements of each of the satellite countries that broke away from Soviet rule. When the Solidarity trade union in Poland finally entered into negotiations with the government, its first request was for equal time on state TV. Jerzy Urban, the government spokesman, responded, "We will give you the ZOMO (riot police) before we give you TV." But after Solidarity won ninety-nine of the one hundred freely contested Senate seats in Poland's first open election, the movement gained control over the state media, and used it effectively to organize the final overthrow of General Wojciech Jaruzelski's government in 1990. In Romania protesters marched not on Parliament but to the TV Center, where a long battle raged with security forces, all of it broadcast live. When the revolutionaries won and Ceausescu was killed, the Romanian broadcast studios became the new seat of government.

Similar tales of the mass media becoming active participants in Eastern Europe's liberation could be told for each country. Coverage of one country's protests fueled protests elsewhere. As East Germans watched news reports of thousands of fellow citizens streaming into Hungary and then Austria without interference, they were emboldened to join the revolution.

The Unraveling

As popular rebellions spread throughout Eastern Europe, the question in most people's minds was, "Would the Soviet army crush the dissent in their satellite states as it had in Hungary in 1956?" But in October 1989, just weeks before the fall of the Berlin Wall, President Gorbachev told the United Nations he was dropping the Brezhnev Doctrine, under which the Soviets had asserted their right to intervene. "Everyone must have the freedom to choose," he told the stunned delegates. "There must be no exceptions." The UN General Assembly rose to its feet and cheered.

But as Gorbachev contended with the separation of the Warsaw Pact satellite countries, the forces of national identity were beginning to pull apart his own, as provincial broadcasters in the other Soviet republics tested their independence from Moscow. Long-suppressed ethnic and nationalist forces pushed for change. In the Baltic States and in Georgia and in Ukraine, particularly, national-language programming shoved aside Russian.

After Lithuania had declared its independence from the Soviet Union earlier in 1990, there were endless meetings and rallies in the republic for and against secession. In the early morning hours of January 13, 1991, two columns of armored vehicles entered the capital, Vilnius, and Soviet army troops stormed the TV Center, killing thirteen pro-independence demonstrators who were protecting the station. Footage of peaceful protesters being crushed under the treads of the "people's army" was suppressed by Soviet state television, but independent producers managed to broadcast these iconic images on Leningrad's more independent local channel, which many Muscovites could also see. The killings in Vilnius touched a raw nerve in the budding independence movements in the non-Russian republics.

The Birth of Media Development

In June 1991, after state television refused to broadcast the footage from Vilnius, TV journalists in Moscow went on strike to demand greater freedom and independence on the state news. Prominent journalists and film directors led by Yegor Yakovlev, editor-in-chief of the *Moscow News*, created the Glasnost Defense Fund to support the families of striking TV journalists. Invited to attend its board meeting in Moscow shortly after the fund was formed, I met Manana Aslamazyan for the first time. Aslamazyan was the only woman in the room and the only Glasnost Defense Fund paid staff. It was immediately clear she was the person in charge. A room full of famous and powerful men routinely deferred to her. An Armenian by birth, she was passionate and stubborn and always spoke from her heart. I took Alexey Simonov, a film director and the head of the Glasnost Defense Fund, aside and asked if Internews could hire Aslamazyan to manage our operations in Russia and the other republics. Half joking, I offered to trade my new Macintosh Classic computer for her. The Glasnost Defense Fund had no prospects for continued funding beyond the immediate campaign in support of the striking journalists and with Aslamazyan running Internews, the two organizations would be like one, he thought. He agreed, and the three of us shook hands. Later, I happily handed over my computer.

Largely unnoticed in Moscow, independent pirate television stations launched broadcasts on local airwaves in cities across the vast Soviet Union. As political power ebbed in the center, these local commercial stations grew largely unhindered. In the summer of 1991 Aslamazyan sent six Russian-speaking researchers to scour the land in search of independent, pirate stations. By the time they reported back, they had discovered two hundred new broadcasters—mostly tiny operations that stole programs off satellites or bought smuggled videocassettes from West Germany and, often as not, broadcast them on the centralized cable systems that wired the monstrous Soviet apartment complexes to a single antenna. For a few dollars, someone could turn a videocassette recorder into a cable station capable of reaching a hundred thousand or more people.

Most of the new station owners, however, thought they were the only ones operating like this. In October 1991, the Glasnost Defense Fund organized a conference in Novgorod bringing these new television entrepreneurs together. As the various station owners looked around at each other, they realized they were not alone. Under Aslamazyan's indomitable leadership, the independent media movement took off. She was soon involved in the startup of six hundred Russian commercial television channels and more than a thousand in the rest of the Soviet Union. She led the development of the first association of broadcasters and organized the training of thousands of new journalists.

Independent media flourished as the center of Communist power waned, but political power increasingly depended on control of the airwaves. As Reino Paasilinna observed in his book, *Glasnost and Soviet Television*:

> *Television was discovered to have a power whose existence no one had suspected, or perhaps, in which no one had believed. . . . A*

unique dethroning of political officials took place on the television screen. No important historical events or individuals, nor the party, nor the system, nor even the most carefully fostered beliefs withstood the gaze of public opinion; everything was blown apart or annihilated. People learned about the mechanisms of power, which had been kept in such stringent secrecy. Earlier, changes of such scope would have been impossible without physical violence, but now television became the nation's judge.

Gorbachev's Demise

Desperate to maintain some semblance of control over his increasingly rebellious republics, Gorbachev negotiated a treaty with eight of them, including Yeltsin's Russia. For the Russian hardliners who had done everything to sabotage Gorbachev's reforms, it was too much of a threat. At 6:29 a.m. on June 19, 1991, the morning before the treaty was to be signed, Soviet television suddenly announced that Mikhail Gorbachev, on vacation in the Crimea, would be unable to perform his duties as president because of unspecified health problems. An hour later huge T-54 tanks and armored personnel carriers from the Kantomirovsky Tank Division rumbled ominously towards the Kremlin. *Swan Lake* played on the state television channels.

I was in California when I got a call from Sasha Lyubimov, one of the young hosts of *Vzglyad*, who was in hiding. He was cut off from his network's equipment, and wanted to know if Internews had access to a television camera he could borrow. It so happened we had a Betacam stuck in customs. Somehow Lyubimov managed to get it freed, and Leningrad TV courageously broadcast his reports.

On the morning of the military/ KGB coup against

the government, Boris Yeltsin went to the White House, Russia's Parliament building, and issued a defiant call for a general strike over a portable radio transmitter. Yeltsin urged people to surround the White House and protect the Russian government. Tens of thousands of people responded and erected barricades around the building. When a tank battalion of the Tamanskaya Motorized Infantry Division arrived at the White House, its commander defied orders from his Soviet commanders and instead declared his loyalty to Yeltsin and his Russian government. Yeltsin emerged and climbed on one of the tanks to address the crowd, a moment that captured the attention of the world. In a sign that the coup leaders did not have full control, the episode was surprisingly included on state TV's Channel One evening news.

Two days later, the coup collapsed. Gorbachev soon returned to Moscow, but Yeltsin had proven to be the person in charge. On August 24, two months later, Mikhail Gorbachev resigned as general secretary of the Party. By December 1991, the USSR formally dissolved.

The Fall of Independent Television

Yeltsin's Russia was a wild west of opportunism and despair. The media, which under Soviet rule had been tasked as the overseer of public morality, turned into the mouthpiece of unbridled capitalism. With its military discipline and narrow ideology, the rigidly ordered Communist society was ruthlessly dismantled, and replaced by the god of profit and commerce. The new freedom had few boundaries—one television news program even featured a TV anchor doing a striptease while she read the day's news. Competition for audience share and advertising dollars, however, rapidly raised the quality of programming, introducing Western-style game shows, soap operas, and sitcoms.

Local, independent media proliferated and grew in size and sophistication. Offering multiple channels in each city, they outdrew the local state television system. Oligarchs purchased television stations and built networks to protect their wealth and enhance their political influence. With financial backing from Ted Turner, Eduard Sagalayev, the creator of *12th Floor* and *Vzglyad*, launched TV-6, the first independent television network in Russia, soon followed by the Independent Broadcast System (IBS) that Aslamazyan helped organize.

If TV-6 and the IBS posed a challenge to existing state television, a new channel, NTV, founded in 1993, conquered it. In just two years NTV claimed a potential audience of seventy million viewers across all eleven time zones. Four of the six top-rated news programs were on NTV. Competition was fierce. By the end of 1993, state subsidies for the two government broadcasters, Channel One and Russian TV, had dropped precipitously, with oligarchs and politicians fighting over the spoils. As Ellen Mickiewicz wrote in *Changing Channels*, "Moscow went to war over Ostankino (the state broadcasting center) in 1993. These two channels, especially Channel One, were thought to hold the fate of the country, to save or lose Russia in election after election and in crisis after crisis. Television was still the obsession of the administration in power and its adversaries."

At the beginning of October 1993, I was in Kiev, Ukraine for a meeting with Aslamazyan and some of the key station managers from independent channels throughout the former Soviet Union. Suddenly, someone ran in and yelled, "There are tanks in Moscow moving on the White House." Tension had been building in a power struggle between Yeltsin and the Russian parliament, which voted to impeach him after he arbitrarily dissolved the legislature. Large crowds had gathered outside the parliament to protect Vice President Aleksandr Rutskoi, the leader of the rebellion, who was named acting president. On October 3, demonstrators broke through police barricades and stormed the Parliament building. In an iconic moment, Rutskoi came out on a balcony and told the protesters, "You are at the wrong address. Go to Ostankino," a few miles away. The locus of revolution was the TV tower.

We all scurried to a television mounted on the wall. Tuning in to Russian State TV, broadcasting from Ostankino, we watched live coverage of an exchange of automatic weapons fire on the ground floor of the TV center where we all had been innumerable times. Then the screen switched to footage of Russian Army tanks shooting at the Parliament and a long column of tanks slowly moving to the city center; then back to live coverage from Ostankino, broadcast literally from the floor above the fighting.

More than five hundred miles away, in Kiev, half the people watching with me were from Moscow and had left family and co-workers behind. It was frightening, a personal nightmare playing out before our eyes on live television. My colleagues from Moscow immediately prepared to rush to the train station in an effort to get back to the Russian capital. Many were crying and frantically trying to reach their loved ones. One hundred and forty-three people were killed in the battle for Ostankino. In the end, President Yeltsin and his Russian Channel prevailed. But the battle to control the airwaves had only begun.

In the aftermath of the fighting over Ostankino, powerful

business groups competed for their own television networks in what Ivan Zassoursky, a journalist and media historian, calls an "information arms race." "Politics and the mass media were becoming totally intertwined," he wrote in *Media and Power in Post-Soviet Russia,* "making it possible to speak of a media-political system." Political factions formed around separate national channels.

In October 1994, a political thunderclap terrified the new financial elites: the resurrected Communist Party won more than twice the votes of the government's party in the parliamentary elections of 1995. A Communist, Gennady Seleznyov, was elected speaker of the Russian Duma, the lower house of the Russian parliament. This set off a series of events that would mark the end of the "Golden Age of Russian Television."

It was a humiliating defeat for President Yeltsin and struck fear into the hearts of the new moneyed class that had grown rich in the transition from Communism to a market economy. If the revanchist Communists captured the presidency from Yeltsin, the oligarchs realized, they stood to have their fortunes expropriated and possibly worse. Panic seized the ruling class. The fierce infighting between the media-political-industrial cartels came to a sudden halt in a remarkable display of class solidarity as the competing media houses joined to support an ailing and faltering Yeltsin in the coming election, making a mockery of journalistic independence.

Igor Maleshenko, the president of NT V, took over as the chief media advisor for the campaign and together with Yeltsin's daughter, Tatyana Dyachenko, engineered a remarkable makeover of the president. NT V had become the most authoritative news source in Russia, largely from its hard-hitting, professional reporting and its criticisms of the government. But in the face of a real threat of a Communist election victory, NT V and its rivals coordinated their coverage of the campaign, employing American-style, sophisticated polling techniques and flooding the airwaves with messages that the return of the Communists would bring about chaos and civil war.

Maleshenko and Dyachenko also managed to turn the image of their candidate from a doddering old man into a dynamic leader. Suddenly, Yeltsin was seen everywhere: barnstorming the country, mingling with the people, issuing decrees and even dancing onstage. He was transformed back into a man of action like the hero who stood on a tank and defied the military five years before. In the end, the negative advertising campaign against the Communists and a newly invigorated Yeltsin gave the president an impressive thirteenpoint victory.

The media campaign succeeded in saving the Yeltsin presidency and perhaps the free market system in Russia, but it marked the end of an unprecedented period of media freedom. Maleshenko may have intervened with the best of intentions to save democracy, but it was a Faustian bargain. As Alexey Simonov put it, "The press decided that it could put aside part of its freedom, and get it back with interest. But freedom never grows in the bank."

Three years later, when Vladimir Putin succeeded Boris Yeltsin, NTV, despite its popularity, was a billion dollars in debt to the state-owned oil giant, Gazprom, because of expensive infrastructure investments. NTV's owner, Vladimir Gusinsky, went to see the newly appointed President Putin and threatened to take him down in the coming election, if he didn't offer some relief. Putin ignored the threat and won the election with a vicious media campaign on ORT, the newly semi-privatized state Channel One. After the election Putin took his revenge. He ordered Gusinsky arrested for fraud and had him thrown into Butyrskaya Prison. Released three days later, Gusinsky flew to Spain, only to be arrested again and then stripped of his citizenship and sent into exile.

The takeover of NTV and the arrest of Gusinsky gave Putin control over the most important national media networks in the country, and virtually ended political and media pluralism in Russia. With this show of force, Putin soon cowed the remaining oligarchs and consolidated his power. Apparently to send a message to the hundreds of local independent television stations across the country as well, Putin's security forces arrested Manana Aslamazyan, sent her into exile, and closed the Internews office.

The great blossoming of freedom of speech that transformed Russia from the days of Gorbachev's glasnost, that helped bring down Soviet Communism and helped end the Cold War, was over. From 2001 until the present, the Russian media would return to the kind of government model that prevailed in earlier Soviet times. The revolution would not be televised.

FROM STONE AGE
TO TWITTER

Unlike the Soviet Union, which under the Communists used media for propaganda, Afghanistan under the Taliban was a black hole of human freedom. Media of all kinds were essentially banned. After the radical Islamists took over the country in the fall of 1996, Afghanistan devolved into a land of intolerance and fanaticism wracked by endless internecine war. Cut off from the rest of the world, it became a primitive cultural wasteland. Women were largely confined to their homes. Girls were not allowed to go to school, while boys were taught only the rote recitation of the Quran in a language they didn't understand. Ancient cultural heritage sites were destroyed, museums ransacked, books burned and music and dance forbidden. But since the allied forces chased the Taliban from power in October 2001, Afghanistan has become an extraordinary example of how, thanks largely to media and new digital technologies, a fantastically undeveloped society can leapfrog to modernity in a single decade.

Given the media's focus on the military clash between the Taliban and NATO, it is easy to forget the cultural clash that will more likely determine the long-term future of the country. Two societies now coexist: one modern, young, media-savvy, and connected; the other devout, insular, traditionally misogynous, and resistant to change. The "new Afghanistan" lives in a world whose values, aspirations and identities are largely shaped by an indigenous media that did not exist before 2001. While the immediate future of the country is uncertain at best, as it approaches the 2014 withdrawal of NATO troops, there are reasons to believe that these cultural changes cannot be wholly reversed in the decades to come.

In the Shadow of 9/11

American and international NGOs had come into Afghanistan in the wake of NATO's rout of the Taliban, which was retaliation for the sanctuary and support it had given Osama Bin Laden and Al Qaeda leading up to the terrorist attacks of 9/11. The world was united then in the aftermath of this tragedy. A large coalition of democratic states backed NATO's intervention in support of the United Islamic Front for the Salvation of Afghanistan. The Front was known in the West as the Northern Alliance, a grouping of forces that had continued to fight against the Taliban after the young Islamic fundamentalists, backed by Pakistan, had swept them from power. Their inspiration was the charismatic Ahmad Shah Massoud. He had been assassinated two days before 9/11 by suicide bombers posing as journalists; they had hidden an explosive device inside a video camera. As the Taliban retreated to the mountains and then to sanctuaries inside Pakistan, the Northern Alliance began to form an interim government around the Pashtun leader Hamid Karzai, and the United States jumped into the void with the daunting task of nation building, something President George W. Bush had vowed never to do.

News junkies may recall that when Northern Alliance troops halted their drive on the outskirts of Kabul, John Simpson, the BBC's main foreign affairs correspondent, walked down the gentle slope into the city from the ridge that runs up to the Shomali plain and the spectacular snowcapped peaks of the Hindu Kush thirty miles to the north. "It's an exhilarating feeling to be liberating a city," Simpson declared, the camera following behind as he strode, arms outstretched, cutting a swath through the jubilant and welcoming throng. It was a bit of punkish British humor, but a media invasion indeed followed closely behind him. Decimated by five weeks of intense, targeted bombing of a firepower they had never imagined, all but a small pocket of the Taliban had slipped away the previous night. There was hardly any fighting in the Afghan capital that day. Around the globe, thousands of TV and radio channels interrupted normal programming to bring images of happy bearded warriors shooting into the air, smiling young men defying the Taliban ban and shaving their beards for the first time in years, and spontaneous singing and dancing in the streets.

Alex Thompson of Independent Television News reported outbreaks of "joy and the simple act of flying a kite again; that great Afghan passion which the Taliban tried so hard to stamp out. And in music coming from the few bazaars open today, and, of course, in the crowds gathering to cheer parties of Alliance soldiers wherever they appeared as they began entering the city this morning. There was a roundabout near the city center, which became speaker's corner as people gave vent to their relief."

Most of the world saw all this, hour after rolling hour on whatever channel we zapped to, or blazoned across the front pages and on the newsstands day after day—except for the vast majority of Afghans. Other than what unfolded in front of their eyes—fragments of reality, often scary, usually without explanation or context—the people most affected had little clue as to what was going on. There was no Afghan newspaper sporting the headline "Taliban Gone!" for the simple reason that local newspapers didn't exist. The Taliban had banned them, along with music, perfume, long hair, speaking Persian, soccer, Labor Day, the Internet, and flared trousers.

The media darkness was not total. Some inside Afghanistan got news of what was happening from international broadcasters such as the BBC's Persian and Pashto language services, Voice of America, Deutsche Welle and others, but none of these had been produced inside the country. The Internet and mobile phones had not yet arrived and citizens had to travel to neighboring countries to make international phone calls. In the center of Kabul, at the television studios of Radio Sedaye Shari'a, the Taliban's radio station (which exclusively broadcast non-stop Quran and other Islamic programming), an imposing woman named Jamila Mujahed earned her own footnote in Afghan history just by walking onto the set, unscripted, to announce that the Taliban had fallen. That it was a female journalist to make this pronouncement signaled the new government supported a more open and tolerant culture. But it was of more symbolic than of any practical importance, since hardly anyone in the country had television sets. The signal, when there was diesel for the generator to power the transmitter, did not extend even over the city of Kabul. It is a fair bet that if you are reading this book, you knew more about what was going on in 2001 than those in Afghanistan who were shaving their beards or flying their kites or wondering if they would survive the night.

With its first grant from the Office of Transition Initiatives (OTI), part of the United States Agency for International Development (USAID), Internews worked to help rehabilitate Afghan Television and Radio (ATR), the country's state-run broadcast service. However, it soon became apparent that the state broadcaster was firmly under the control of Marshall Fahim and the Northern Alliance and would not become a source of reliable news that could reunite the country. Transforming state-run broadcasters is almost always an impossible task in any country transitioning to democracy.

A signal survey Internews conducted throughout the country revealed that less than half of Afghanistan's population could even receive ATR's signal; therefore, with funding from OTI, we decided to build FM stations in areas outside the capital that remained in media darkness. This local radio network was literally created from the ground up.

On the Ground with Media Development

As I drove in from the Kabul airport on a cool, dry October evening in 2003, the grotesque skeletons of bombed-out buildings were sobering reminders of the challenges we were facing. This was a country cut off from the outside world. Internews had come here in 2001 on the heels of NATO's rout of the Taliban with a mission to train new journalists and establish local radio stations. Given our experiences in setting up independent television and radio outlets in dozens of other developing countries, we were convinced that information and civic education could be the drivers that would bring peace, prosperity, and democracy to this forsaken land. Military might can defeat an enemy, but only media can transform a culture.

The next morning, en route to visit Sharq radio station in Jalalabad, the largest city in eastern Afghanistan, I was joined by three companions—a driver, an interpreter, and a swashbuckling colleague named Johnny West, our Afghan country director, for whom this perilous drive was just another day at the office. I climbed into the back seat of a twenty-year-old Toyota Corolla that looked like it had been sandblasted. We headed up the road to Jalalabad.

The forty-mile national highway through the Kabul Gorge in Afghanistan is considered one of the most treacherous routes on earth. Vertical rock cliffs tower two thousand feet above the Kabul River and there is scarcely enough room for two cars, let alone trucks, to pass each other. And yet pass they must, as this is the lifeline that brings food and other goods to the capital from the Pashtun east of the country. He who controls the roads of Afghanistan, it is said, controls the nation. At the time of my visit, three years before the reconstruction of the strategic highway, there was no enforcement of driver's license requirements or traffic laws, and few police. The country seemed to revel in the fear it inspired.

We drove up out of the dust and jumble of Kabul as it awoke, through tangles of motorbikes, bicycles and the ubiquitous taxis, and waited with frustration for a long convoy of NATO trucks ferrying Abrams M1 tanks that appeared incongruously like invaders from another planet in this land largely devoid of modern technology. We passed roadside villages made of clay with animals kept in the traditional way, tethered and housed behind barriers of sticks and stones. It was hot during the day and freezing at night. A short distance outside the city, the paved highway abruptly gave way to a rough rocky semblance of a road that corkscrewed its way up the mountain. The landscape was sparse and devastatingly beautiful from a distance, but up close was punctuated by rusting corpses of littered cars and trucks that had crashed or fallen over the steep cliffs. My memory of the drive was that of feeling like a finalist in the World Cup of chicken. Motorists seemed to take perverse pleasure in aiming at the oncoming traffic before passing within millimeters of each other.

From the front seat, West recounted what his instructor had taught him at a hostile-environment training course he had attended. "Forget about the flak jackets, armed guards, and self-defense training," he had counseled. "The single best thing you can do to increase your chances of survival in conflict zones is to wear a seat belt." I looked around the back seat. There weren't any.

In time, we reached the summit at Sarobi where the road mercifully starts to drop down to Jalalabad. Sarobi might be history's metaphor for Afghanistan's past and future, its never-ending dance of beauty and death. It was here 160 years ago that a British and Indian force of 4,500 soldiers and their 12,000 camp followers, led by Major General William Elphinstone, were annihilated on their way to a British garrison at Jalalabad a year after capturing Kabul. Only one British officer from the army, Assistant Surgeon William Brydon, survived and eventually reached his destination.

As we slowly meandered down from the summit atop the Kabul Gorge, my body relaxed a bit. The unspoken apprehension in the car eased. In the back seat our translator was extolling the virtues of Afghan customs while in the front Johnny West was chatting and laughing with our driver in Dari, the second major language in Afghanistan, a close cousin to Farsi.

Johnny West is a quintessential Anglo-Irish romantic in the mold of T.E. Lawrence, at home in any environment, the more exotic the better. Able to converse fluently in eight languages, he has always ventured where other Westerners feared to tread. He would wander the back streets of Kabul after work, occasionally coming upon a smoke-filled den of Sufi mystics where he would stay through the night talking of the wonders of God. He has penetrating blue eyes that are alternately elusive like a prophet's or piercing like a cat burglar's, the effect magnified by wire-rimmed glasses. West is an indomitable force of intellect and stubborn determination, always talking a little faster than anyone else, his mind spinning like the dervishes he loves. I often enjoy listening to him recount the endless stories and the fantastic people he has known. The moment you think you fully grasp one of his mind-bending insights, he is off on something else. Instinctively strategic, he has an uncanny ability to grasp the big picture while obsessing over the minute details of implementation. A former Reuters journalist covering the Arab world, West's fantastic stories convey a ground view of reality only few journalists can capture, but always with an eye over the horizon.

As we traveled on blessedly flat ground past Sarobi, past some camel herders and small boys rolling hoops with sticks amid rusted hulks of Russian oil tankers, our translator said, "This is where those four journalists were kidnapped and killed when they had to stop to change a flat tire." I was familiar with the story. Just before leaving the States for Kabul, I had spoken with an American diplomat who had recently gone to Afghanistan to recover their bodies. He told me the harrowing, but unreported fact, that the men had all been skinned alive. The commander who was thought to have captured them had a savage reputation—once reputed to have bitten off parts of prisoners' bodies.

Within a minute of him saying the word "killed," right on cue came an unforgettable sound. Thud-thud-thud. One of our tires had blown out.

We stepped out of the car gingerly. Little kids quickly surrounded us, eager to see the foreigners. While the driver changed the tire, I did magic tricks—making coins disappear and then reappear behind a boy's ear, pretending to take off my finger—as I carefully surveyed the scene. I kept my eyes on the men, hoping upon hope that their smiles would remain. A man on a motorbike left in a swirl of dust. Was he going to alert others? What were they whispering to each other? Why did that one man look so grim? How nervous was our translator? The kids pulled at my sleeves wanting more tricks, but all I could feel was my heart thumping and the hairs on the back of my neck standing straight. If I could stay calm and relaxed, I said to myself, everyone else will and this will all pass.

Finally, our driver stood up. The last lug nuts had been tightened on the spare and he motioned for us to get in the car. I waved goodbye to the kids.

We drove uneventfully onto Jalalabad, a colorful, sprawling town near the Khyber Pass and the border with Pakistan. Buses and trucks caromed around covered with painted floral designs and festooned with bright beaded lights in a garish cacophony of kitsch, known as jingle art.

Internews had a $1 million grant from OTI to build fourteen independently owned radio stations in a year, a goal no one really believed we could accomplish. Sharq Radio in

Jalalabad was one of those stations. By the time I arrived in October 2003, we were working on building our thirteenth radio station that year and had a staff of one hundred.

Johnny West was in charge of managing the grant. He had to build a team of engineers and technical experts, journalism trainers, and the accountants and program managers who would oversee the distribution of relatively large sums of money in a country with virtually no financial infrastructure. He was aided by Sanjar Qiam, the bright young manager of the run-down hotel where our staff was staying, who was recruited to become our office manager.

Most ex-pats who go to Afghanistan end up falling in love with the country and its people. Many Afghans are guileless, honorable and largely free of pretentiousness. Known for being fierce warriors, they are a remarkably tender people. When an Afghan greets you, it is always with the greatest warmth and respect. It is not at all incongruous that the assassin who killed former President Burhanuddin Rabbani with a bomb hidden in his turban first kissed his victim's hand and hugged him respectfully.

When Johnny West took over as project manager, after the initial two-year leadership of intrepid media missionary George Papagiannis, he assumed one of the most complex jobs imaginable. It was a logistical nightmare freighted with cultural clashes and security threats. One would be hard pressed to find a more difficult environment in which to establish a radio station, let alone fourteen of them. Identifying entrepreneurs willing to take the risk of running a high visibility project like a radio station was just one of the myriad obstacles he faced.

In Jalalabad he recruited a wheeler-dealer named Shafiqullah Shaiq who had a thriving business trading whiskey and other goods to the Taliban before NATO ran them out of town. Shaiq proved relatively reliable and motivated by the prospects of making more money with the Americans than he did with the Taliban. The station, Sharq Radio, 91.3 FM, proved to be hugely popular. To generate income, its disc jockeys would read birthday greetings and love notes on the air for fifty Afghanis, or one US dollar, equal to a day's pay. To make it easier for listeners to convey their requests, the station installed red drop boxes adorned with their logo throughout the city. Just a few years later, the station and its listeners would communicate via SMS text messages.

When we walked into the studio, Shaiq showed off piles and piles of letters the station received from adoring fans each week. After some chitchat, West and Shaiq sat down to talk business.

Internews was then in the process of establishing a central hub in Kabul, run by a local Afghan NGO, that would transmit six hours a day of programming with national and international news in Pashto and Dari that our incipient network badly needed to fill its airtime. Internews exercised no editorial control over the stations' content, but we offered them training in Western-style, factbased journalism, which they eagerly accepted.

Radio Sharq and others like it served as an electronic commons where grievances and community needs were aired. Besides music and news about politics and sports, the station began experimenting with call-in talk shows, a revolutionary innovation in a country deprived of any media under Taliban rule. Sitting in the station's rudimentary studio and listening to a heated discussion between a female caller and a young journalist, I could feel the excitement of a radically new culture of empowerment forming—even though I didn't speak the language. From past experience I knew that communities were elated by this first taste of democracy and the recognition of citizenship that came with it.

The technical obstacles alone for keeping these stations functioning were daunting. Finding replacement parts and skilled engineers were particularly hard. West created a technical support center that miraculously kept them on the air. In the end, though, it was the enormous thirst for information and media that made these stations such a success.

As Shaiq expounded, "We have unleashed a hidden dragon. People here have lived for centuries in fear—fear to show their face, fear to say what they thought. Now their voices are being broadcast throughout the city. It is like watching a corpse come to life."

Shafiqullah Shaiq would go on to become an Afghan version of a media mogul, creating a network with a television station and three radio stations, including an all-women's channel, a film company, a commanding presence in Jalalabad's social media space, and a newspaper. Radio Sharq and its sister stations formed the foundations for a civil society in Jalalabad, covering local news, offering a forum for politicians, citizen journalists, and bloggers, as well as a platform for the examination of public policy issues by experts and citizens. The resilience of civil society in the midst of a horrific civil war is a testament to the Afghan people's yearning for normality. It is community-based stations like Radio Sharq, as much as Afghanistan's army, which will determine Afghanistan's fate after NATO withdraws in 2014.

But independent radio stations like Radio Sharq did not appear in the immediate aftermath of NATO's rout of the Taliban, as one might expect. In previous post-conflict situations, such as in East Timor and Kosovo, commercial and nonprofit community radio had flourished. In Afghanistan, a full year after it was liberated, this simply had not happened. On the surface conditions seem similar: a new government, a new set of freedoms, and international funding to support such initiatives. Besides the fear of assuming such a powerful public role, another reason for this absence may have been the lack of influence media had in bringing about regime change in Afghanistan. Unlike other political revolutions in East and Central Europe, Indonesia, and Peru, where media played a crucial role in political change, in Afghanistan media were almost irrelevant to the fall of the Taliban. Change in those other countries came about to a great extent because of internal pressures from an activist media and intellectuals. Change in Afghanistan, however, came about through external force, while most journalists in the country remained on the sidelines over the decades.

But media in Afghanistan were about to become a powerful force for social change in a country that seemed almost immune to modernization. In 2003, with an all-Afghan staff directed by Mirweis Social, a young Afghan journalist, Internews established a national radio service called Salaam Watandar, or "Hello Countrymen," modeled on America's National Public Radio, which provided national and international news and current affairs programming to a network of local stations. The community stations, like Radio Sharq, were responsible for contributing local stories to fill the daily feed from Kabul. In a country without a functioning national media, the aggregation of these local stories from different regions contributed to building a sense of national identity, particularly important in a country like Afghanistan with so many tribal and linguistic divisions. Local programs were sent on CDs by bus to Kabul and the assembled news feed was transmitted by satellite back to the stations. In a remarkably few short years content would be transmitted using innovative Voice Over Internet Protocols.

Welcome to the Twenty-first Century

The newest station to join the network after Radio Sharq was Radio Miliy Pagham in the Pul-e Alam District of Logar Province, about fifty miles south of Kabul, the scene of some of the most intense fighting between Soviet troops and the Mujahideen in the early 1980s. On the way to its opening in October 2003, West and I stopped at the home of Tariq Usman, the new station manager, a radio engineer and a former resistance fighter who had taken up arms with Gulbuddin Hekmatyar, a controversial rebel military commander notorious for killing civilians and his own allies. He was once a darling of the CIA, but Hekmatyar had always hated America and, after 9/11, aligned himself with the Taliban. Usman, who had also worked for the Taliban as the webmaster for its Foreign Ministry before 2001, was now a delegate to the Loya Jirga, the traditional tribal gathering called to draft Afghanistan's new constitution. We sat in the patio of his modest compound drinking tea. Chickens pecked at corn in the dirt around us. Usman had no fingers on his left hand, the result of a mortar shell. He was a kind and jovial man who clearly commanded the respect of everyone around him.

Soon we headed out to the radio station. It lay on a desolate ridge where a famous battle had been fought between Soviet forces and the Mujahideen. The ground was still littered with spent shell casings. At the top of the hill, Usman had erected a small, square, mud-brick building. Inside was a modern soundboard, editing and broadcasting equipment, and a separate room made soundproof with egg cartons and foam tacked to the walls. A one-hundred-foot tower had been welded to the top of the building.

This was the first radio station in the province—ever. The gear was minimal but technically up-to-date and an obvious source of pride to Usman and his staff. Inside, a radio announcer and a sound engineer whom we had trained were beaming with excitement. A large crowd began to form around the little mud studio, anxiously awaiting the start of the ceremonies. Silhouetted on the surrounding hills, spaced every twenty meters, were soldiers cradling Kalashnikovs.

We walked down from the stone and cartridge-strewn slope to a large tent that shielded the local dignitaries from the sun—the general in charge of the Afghan Army, the mullahs, the chief of police and other local luminaries, all men. I took my place next to an elderly blind man with a long white beard dressed in flowing garb who sat transfixed with anticipation. The two hundred wooden chairs assembled under the tent were quickly filled. A simple microphone stood in front. A wizened old man with a turban larger than his head stepped up to the mike and began reciting poetry. People smiled, swayed and bobbed their heads in appreciation. West was next. He spoke with apparent ease for about ten minutes in Pashto, the old men nodding in approval. Then he seamlessly translated for himself into Dari. It was quite a performance.

And then something truly magical happened. At the appointed moment, the radio signal came to life. As I looked around at the men in their baggy *salwar kameez*, long overshirts and turbans, I noticed two teenage boys holding portable radios to their ears. Their faces were suddenly filled with wonder. These boys were not only listening to radio for the first time; this was also the first time they had heard music! The Taliban would have chopped off their hands.

Two Steps Forward, One Step Back

Four years after it opened, Radio Miliy Pagham was burned to the ground by the Taliban, but the community soon came together to help rebuild it. This kind of support is likely the main reason why such attacks are relatively rare. But building a community radio station in the middle of a war is undoubtedly dangerous. The same year, in June 2007, gunmen entered the house of Zakia Zaki, an Afghan journalist who was the owner and manager of Radio Sada-i-Sulh, or Peace Radio in Parwan, north of Kabul. They shot her seven times in the chest and head, killing her while she lay asleep in her bedroom, her baby left uninjured next to her. A respected and inspirational community leader and headmistress of a high school for girls, Zaki, thirty-five years old, described Peace Radio as "a community home for the residents, the only place where they dare to express themselves freely."

Compared with other international intervention efforts, such as building infrastructure, upgrading public health services, or modernizing agriculture, media development projects are quickly realized at relatively low cost and with immediate impact. It is astonishing to see the effect a simple call-in show elicits in a community that has never experienced such a thing. The need for recognition, the need to be seen for who one is and what one thinks, is the core of human dignity. When people in a country like Afghanistan can hear their voices and express their opinions without fear, it transforms the culture.

I sometimes marvel at the game-changing leaps in recent history. I try to explain to my own kids what it was like to hide under a desk during air raid drills when our country lived in fear of a thermonuclear Armageddon. They can't possibly understand what my generation experienced, hard as they might try. The same is true of the generation of people who lived under Soviet Communism and their children. Now in Afghanistan, just a decade after Taliban rule was overthrown, teenagers remember little of what life was actually like in that darker time. The war goes on and the immediate future looks grim, but for many young Afghans life under Taliban rule is just another set of stories their parents tell them. And the boys who were listening to their first radio program not so long ago are now probably busy surfing the Internet.

Seeing Is Believing

John Langlois, our main funder at OTI, felt strongly that the country needed a more sophisticated commercial radio and television station in Kabul that could raise the bar for all the others. He expected there'd be resistance from the Ministry of Communication, which feared more independent media, so he searched for someone with enough clout to get a license.

Saad Mohseni is a garrulous, congenial man with short, curly dark hair, black square glasses and a distinct Australian accent. He and his brothers—Wajma, Jahid, and Zaid— were sons of a respected Afghan diplomat who had fled the country in 1982 and moved his family to Australia. The Mohseni brothers had a modest but successful investment company, Moby Capital. With the fall of the Taliban they saw an opportunity to do business in their homeland and began looking into the licensing requirements for a radio station in the capital. Saad Mohseni told Langlois he would be willing to invest $300,000 in such a start-up, but the venture would require more than a half a million. Langlois was impressed when he heard this. These were the kinds of entrepreneurs who could build a first-class station and they were willing to put in some of their own capital to boot. So, OTI gave them a grant of $228,000 to make up the difference and in 2003, a few months before I arrived there, they launched Kabul-based Arman FM. The brothers chose a format of Western, Afghan, and Indian music and the station quickly attracted a large audience and was soon the most popular channel in the country. A year later the Mohsenis started Tolo TV, which means "Dawn" in Dari. The US government invested heavily this time, with $2.5 million for transmitters and infrastructure, while the Mohsenis invested another $3.5 million for operating expenses.

It was a smart investment. Tolo TV is not only a financial success, it is also a culturally disruptive technology that fundamentally challenges traditional social and political mores and is opening a window to modernity. Its programming is a mix of Indian soap operas, music videos, imported films, news, and current affairs. Women appear alongside men and even compete against them on game shows. Indian soap operas feature women without veils and journalists aggressively report on government incompetence, voter fraud, and rampant corruption.

Looking back at Tolo TV's success, it is easy to see the decision to invest in it as a no-brainer. But introducing contemporary content and provocative styles into a deeply devout and traditional culture like Afghanistan's can easily cause a backlash. How to push the normative boundaries of a society without insulting its cultural values requires skill and sensitivity that foreigners are unlikely to have—a point often made in arguing for local media development over any "Made in the USA" social marketing. This holds as well for public health campaigns and public diplomacy. Local almost always trumps foreign.

In a wide variety of countries around the world experiencing a new media reality, one notices a universal attraction to higher production values and, particularly, faster pacing. Audiences, without much prior TV exposure, are drawn to the quality of the programming almost as much as the content. Tolo TV's production values are high compared to any of its competitors, which help it overcome objections from conservative religious factions to the content. While religious conservatives are outraged by seeing young boys and girls dancing together, legs and shoulders bare, the overwhelming majority of TV viewers in Kabul—over 65 percent by some estimates—tune in. "Watching a woman with half-naked breasts and a man and a woman sucking each other's lips on TV, like on Tolo, is not acceptable," wrote one critic. And it is not just the mullahs who felt threatened. The political class is unnerved by Tolo's investigative journalism, live coverage and exposure of abuse within the central government. Threats of arrests and intimidation are constant, but Tolo's steadfast refusal to compromise and the popularity of its programs give it a constituency that matches those of the politicians who want to shut it down.

Richard Holbrooke, the US special representative for Afghanistan and Pakistan before his untimely death in December 2010, described the challenge that Tolo TV posed to Afghan traditionalists:

"The country is highly illiterate, highly religious, and highly traditional. And Saad [Mohseni] is appealing to and creating a new young group of people in the urban areas. There's brilliance to what he's doing, but it's also risky. It's a drama. I can't imagine any other country in the world where it would be played out with this much intensity."

The clash of cultures that Benjamin Barber described in his seminal book *Jihad vs. McWorld* has become part of daily life in Afghanistan. Barber explains how educated classes and young people in particular crave participation in the globalization of entertainment and financial opportunity while fundamentalists fight to preserve the religious orthodoxy from the time of the prophets. Tolo, and to a somewhat lesser extent most of the new media in the country, introduced the values of modern democracies into a society that, just three years before, had been insulated by the religious fanaticism of the Taliban with their rigid two-thousand-year-old morality. Traditional lines of authority within families and in the larger society were incongruent with the social relations that people saw day in and day out on television. Models of behavior were changing.

Perhaps no change was as profound or disruptive as the emerging new status of women. Ken Auletta, in a 2010 *New Yorker* article about Saad Mohseni, observed:

The status of women in Afghanistan is being transformed by the media. Young girls watch soap operas and assert themselves at home, or refuse to wear burkas or accept arranged marriages. Tolo's lifestyle shows have introduced boys and girls to modern fashions and hairstyles, and to modern standards of personal hygiene. Forty percent of Moby's employees are women, and Mohseni believes that, when his radio and TV stations placed women on the same set with men, the format allowed people to think a woman can have a conversation with a man. Maybe women have views. And maybe women are smart. It elevated women to an equal status with men. And it allowed men not to be so judgmental of women.

Tolo TV has its share of detractors in addition to the religious and political leaders. Some argue that the TV station compromises too much with the authorities or not enough, others think it is too culturally provocative or that it favors one faction or another; but few can deny it has caused seismic tremors in traditional Afghan society. Popular in Kabul and other urban centers, it is less so in the rural heartland of Afghanistan, as one might expect. Tolo TV began as a Dari-language station, since that was the Mohsenis' mother tongue and is most spoken in the capital. In 2006 the brothers launched a Pashto-language version of Tolo, Lemar (Sun) TV. Moby Capital, the parent company, now owns an advertising agency, a television and movie production company, a music-recording company, and a magazine, *Afghan Scene*, in addition to its radio and television stations. In 2009, in a joint venture with Rupert Murdoch's News Corporation, it launched the Farsi1 satellite network aimed at Iran.

On Thursday nights, a third of Afghanistan's population is glued to the TV to watch Tolo's most popular program, *Afghan Star*, an Afghan version of *American Idol*. Afghan citizens from all classes and ethnicities compete before a frenzied live audience to choose among the three finalists—invariably a Pashtun, a Tajik, and a Hazara—for a $5,000 prize and a recording contract, a rare moment when televised national unity trumps ethnic divisions. Winners are chosen by the judges, the audience, and, remarkably, by SMS text messages sent from mobile phones throughout the country. In a recent finale, three hundred thousand votes were cast this way.

The Road to Modernity

The text messaging results are a window onto something much bigger. The one free market commodity that has any chance of outperforming opium production in Afghanistan is mobile telephony. Although in 2012 only a measly 4 percent of Afghans are connected to the Internet—it costs about $1,000 to establish service in Kabul—the number of cell phone owners has increased dramatically. As of 2012 there were 20.4 million mobile phone users in a population of 29 million; that number is growing by 16 percent a year. Over half the homes in Afghanistan now have access and two-thirds of cell phone users are texting. Mobile technology is the largest taxpaying industry in Afghanistan, accounting for 15 percent of government revenue. Next to agriculture, it is the biggest employer—and undeniably the single greatest economic success story in the country since the fall of the Taliban. As we are seeing around the world, mobile telephony is creating its own disruptive narrative in Afghanistan. Those cell phones put a never-before-imagined power in the hands of users, a power they can experience in near real-time as the tally of votes in the *Afghan Star* contest attests. What is next?

Already, mobile telephony has become a factor in the balance of power between the Afghan people and terrorists and insurgents. Admiral Greg Smith recounted to *The Boston Globe* how US officials meeting on the rooftop terrace of Ambassador Karl Eikenberry's Kabul residence had a *Eureka!*

moment when he spread out two maps. One highlighted pockets of insurgent control; the other marked mobile phone towers. Where the Taliban's presence was strongest, phone coverage was weakest, crippled by their sabotage of the towers. "We found that Afghans in the most troubled, insurgent-held areas lived in information wastelands dominated by militant propaganda," one officer said. "If villagers and security forces can't communicate, that allows terrorist safe havens to thrive."

But it is not really as simple as that. The Taliban need to communicate with cell phones as well. Indeed, they are increasingly making sophisticated use of mobile phone videos to spread their propaganda. It is noteworthy that when the Taliban issued a *fatwa* demanding that mobile towers be switched off or risk being blown up, they quickly backtracked and amended the order to apply only to overnight operations, so as not to antagonize people. The Taliban, too, it seems, must also try and win hearts and minds.

Mobile phones are becoming engrained in the fabric of Afghan life and, while still in its infancy, mobile telephony will increasingly become the main driver of the economy, social change and possibly even politics and government. Because per-minute usage rates are relatively expensive—about four Afghanis or eight US cents a minute, making the cost of a one-hour conversation equivalent to three days' wages—users have favored SMS text messaging. Innovative uses of text messaging have proliferated, in no small part because Roshan, the largest telecommunications company, owned by the Aga Khan Fund for Economic Development, has cooperated with NGOs experimenting with new applications of SMS for development. There are pilot programs that provide farmers with access to commodity prices through text messages, help lines to report instances of domestic violence, and even an ambitious project called Silk Road that is creating an e-registry of land disputes.

One great impediment to rolling out many of these pilot programs, however, is the extremely low literacy rate in the country—about 70 percent of the population is illiterate. But even that can be overcome with an interactive voice response system (IVR) that allows users to choose from a menu of options delivered by voice commands. In a country like Afghanistan, IVRs are an essential technology that should be incorporated into every application for the general public. IVRs have already been deployed in an SMS news service and an election monitoring and reporting program in Afghanistan and in a variety of other countries where literacy rates are low.

Clearly, cell phones are here to stay. But what of social networking and Internet connectivity that has unleashed so much energy and change in other parts of the world? That, too, is part of Afghanistan's turbo-charged journey back from the Stone Age. Because broadband is expensive and Internet use is so low, social networking sites were late in gaining popularity in the country. But as the Internet user base has begun to expand and as young people in particular watched the Arab Spring unfold in fellow Muslim countries, interest is surging. Facebook membership, though among the lowest in the world in terms of total users, now has one of the fastest rates of growth when viewed as a percentage of the population. A new service called Paywast offers a Facebook-type social networking experience entirely through SMS text messaging. This convergence is tailor-made for Afghanistan.

Youth in Afghanistan today (particularly women) speak of the "social media war" as they discuss issues that are too provocative for even the most liberal broadcast media. "Where traditional media are weak, that is where social media step in," said Abdul Mujeeb Khalvatgar, the executive director of the Afghan media advocacy group Nai. Internet cafes are spreading to towns and cities throughout the country as young people embrace the freedom to speak their minds. According to a July 2012 Reuters report, "The austere Taliban banned Internet use to stop people viewing what they derided as vulgar, immoral and anti-Islamic material, although they are now among many groups using social networking to communicate and promote their message." But for most young people in the country, "the use of social media has mainly been confined to combating conservative cultural norms such as limited women's rights, which are more difficult for mainstream media to confront without provoking a backlash."

A final outgrowth of mobile telephony could eventually prove to have the most significant impact of all on Afghan society: mobile money. Pioneered in Kenya by the fantastically successful M-Pesa program, the Afghan M-Paisa service (*pesa* means "money" in Swahili, as does *paisa* in Dari), introduced by Rosan in partnership with Vodaphone, allows users to deposit and withdraw cash from mobile-based accounts, pay bills, secure microfinance loans, purchase goods with e-currency, and transfer money between users with their mobile phones. After each transaction, users immediately receive an SMS confirming the amount exchanged. Mobile money has the potential to transform Afghanistan from a cash economy—an astonishing 97 percent of the people remain "unbanked"—to a mobile money e-commerce system. Banking with mobile phones also circumvents the security problems hindering the spread of bank branches.

Transparency International's Corruption Perceptions Index ranks countries according to the view its citizens have of the degree of corruption found there. Afghanistan is considered the second-most corrupt nation on earth, just ahead of Somalia. By some estimates, up to 40 percent of the economy is siphoned off by bribes. Many observers of Afghanistan place corruption ahead of drugs and terrorism as the most intractable problem facing the country. Proponents of mobile money tout its potential to tackle this monster, often citing a 2009 test in which the Afghan National Police paid salaries through mobile telephones rather than in cash. It immediately found at least 10 percent of its payments had been going to ghost policemen who didn't exist; middlemen in the police hierarchy were pocketing the difference. In Wardak province, fifty officers reported receiving 30 percent larger payments with the program than they had previously and about twenty days sooner.

Despite the obvious success of the experiment, the practice has been slow to be adopted because it threatens the entrenched corruption among senior commanders. Mobile money could be an instant fix to this endemic problem found throughout Afghan politics and society, but only if there is the political will at the top to challenge the system. Presently there is not, but perhaps pressure from below can alter the dynamic for the better. Changes like mobile money, which affect systems of privilege and power, may evolve slowly, but in their aggregate constitute a radical new framework touching every aspect of the status quo.

We Will Never Go Back

When a country undergoes a transformative upheaval like Afghanistan did after the Taliban were overthrown, citizens experience such changes mainly through the media. Media are the common denominator of modern life, the collective eyes and ears of a community. The state of media in any country is a perfect reflection of that country's socio-political reality—for better or for worse. But it is also more than that. Disruptive technologies in the telecommunications sphere can also open up new spaces in culture and society. Media are the advance force in globalization's transformation of traditional societies.

Masood Farivar, an acute observer of media in Afghanistan, who took over as general manager of *Salaam Watandar* radio in 2007, has one of those "made for Hollywood" success stories. The son of well-educated parents, he escaped Afghanistan with his family to Pakistan as refugees from the Soviet occupation in 1983 when he was thirteen. He attended madrassas, joined the Hezb-I-Islami Party at eighteen and fought against the Soviets at Tora Bora. There, a British convert to Islam with the *nom de guerre* of Karimullah, a graduate of Eton who had worked as a Wall Street trader before joining the Mujahideen, helped Farivar get into an elite prep school in New Jersey and then into Harvard, from which he graduated in 1994. Farivar is a devout Muslim, temperamentally conservative. He mourns the loss of traditions of respect and the breakdown of family values that seem inevitable with the onslaught of modernity.

"When my grandfather would enter a room, we would never think of not standing and kissing his hand," he lamented. "Afghans are believers, people of faith. But the way things have been going for the last couple of years does not inspire a lot of confidence in the future. If Afghanistan is going to survive as a land where freedom and tradition can coexist, it will only come from the media."

I asked him what would happen to the media if there were ever a negotiated settlement with the Taliban. "Media is one thing that the Afghan people will insist is non-negotiable," he smiled. "We will never go back."

THE DICTATOR'S DILEMMA

The very concept of a "liberal dictatorship" is something of an oxymoron. Free speech and authoritarian rule exist in opposition to each other. But there are degrees of each that stretch from the absolute dictatorship of North Korea to the largely unregulated speech of most Western democracies. As mentioned, the best judge of the degree of a country's freedom is the state of its media. An authoritarian ruler may choose to liberalize the media in the hopes of modernizing the economy; but he does so at his peril. This is the "dictator's dilemma." When citizens have access to information and the right to speak, but are denied the opportunity to freely elect their leaders, the country is ripe for revolution.

Both Eduard Shevardnadze in Georgia and General Pervez Musharraf in Pakistan wanted to take their countries into the modern information age and compete in the global marketplace by opening their media. Had either left office without being pushed out by popular uprisings, this would have been their legacy. But the forces they unleashed ultimately devoured them.

In Myanmar, as we'll see in the next chapter, the ruling military junta liberalized the media, to virtually everyone's surprise; but President Thein Sein did so in conjunction with a new constitution and wide political reforms, which may allow Myanmar to escape the "dictator's dilemma." China, on the other hand, has kept state-ownership and control over traditional mass media, but has liberalized much of its social media. Unlike Georgia or Pakistan, however, China's ruling party has no organized opposition and the outcome of its own "dictator's dilemma" remains uncertain.

Georgia's "Rose Revolution"

To describe Eduard Shevardnadze as a "liberal dictator," as many do, is perhaps an overstatement, though a democrat he was not. The former foreign minister of the Soviet Union, Shevardnadze was one of the leading reformers who greatly influenced President Gorbachev's policies of glasnost and perestroika. When he resigned as foreign minister of the USSR in December 1990, warning of an imminent coup by disaffected hardliners, he already had his sights set on a return to political power in his native Georgia. His election in Georgia's 2000 presidential election, however, was secured with massive vote rigging and his rule was marred by unbridled nepotism and corruption. Although he allowed the licensing of private broadcasters, when they opposed him, he turned against them.

The story of Shevardnadze's undoing begins with Erosi Kitsmarishvili, a burly man with a stubby beard, a large avuncular face, narrow eyes, and an indomitable determination. Trained as a pediatrician, he tried starting a private insurance company after Georgia gained its independence, but had little success. With two of his best friends, Kitsmarishvili applied for a license to start a commercial television station in the small town of Rustavi just outside the capital, Tbilisi. None of them knew anything about running a television operation, but Kitsmarishvili thought it would be a cost-effective way to promote his new insurance venture.

In June 1994, he and his friends began broadcasting from two tiny rooms in a local hotel. The Rustavi Insurance Company soon went belly up, leaving him with only the television business, Rustavi-2. He was a fast learner, however, and gobbled up every journalism and management-training course he could find. "We were so naïve," Kitsmarishvili told me in a 2012 interview. "We thought television was going to be very easy to organize. We had no idea what television and broadcasting required and how the business works. Then we attended a seminar for local television start-ups in the Caucasus and we began to get a more serious understanding of television as a business—how to manage, sell commercials, and organize the newsroom."

Two years later, Rustavi-2 moved its operations to Tbilisi, hoping to tap into the much larger advertising market there. But after just one month of broadcasting, the Ministry of Communications, fearful of the station's independence, shut it down and took away its license. That lasted a year. Once allowed back on, it began to grow at a phenomenal rate and by 2000 had become the top commercial television channel in Georgia and the only one with a national reach. The owners invested heavily in purchasing foreign programs, which they translated into Georgian, and bought the rights to the European soccer championships. They produced the first game show in Georgia, *Who Wants to be a Millionaire?* modeled on the British series. The channel was the first in the country to send its journalists to conflicts overseas. Georgians took pride in seeing homegrown reporters broadcasting from the war in Kosovo, an unprecedented opportunity for viewers to watch international news coverage on a local independent television station instead of one of the Russian government channels. Rustavi-2 also aired investigative reports, sometimes with footage from hidden cameras, exposing secret arms deals by government officials with Chechen rebels in the Pankisi Gorge and corruption among President Shevardnadze's family members, the Interior Ministry and others. Rustavi-2 journalists were arrested or beaten, shots were fired at the station and libel and defamation cases were instigated as the government constantly harassed and threatened the broadcaster.

In 1999 Shevardnadze approached Kitsmarishvili and suggested he sell Rustavi-2 to Badri Patarkatsishvili, a partner of Rupert Murdoch's. There were on and off again negotiations, and by July 2001, Kitsmarishvili finally had agreed to sell. On July 26, though, on the very day they were to sign the papers, Giorgi Sanaia, the young anchor of *Night Courier*, the highest rated news program in the country, was killed, shot in the head at close range in his apartment with a 9mm pistol. Just three nights earlier, Sanaia had aired a tough segment about political corruption, smuggling and other illegal activities in the Pankisi Gorge. Interior Minister Kakha Targamadze had publically accused him of subversion and threatened to shut down the station.

Popular suspicion as to who was behind the assassination naturally focused on Sanaia's investigative reports, suggesting the complicity of either top politicians or criminals. A few months later, on December 6, police arrested a former police officer, Grigol Khurtsilava, after a ballistic analysis traced the murder weapon to him. Acting on his confession, police found the gun and the keys to Sanaia's apartment. Khurtsilava was then officially charged with Sanaia's murder. But doubts about the murder persisted.

(More than a decade later I asked Kitsmarishvili what he suspected was behind the killing. "It's an untold story," he told me. "I have never mentioned this publicly because I had no proof. But it is very interesting that he was killed the same day that we had planned to sell the station. If Patarkasishvili would have taken over, the balance inside the government would have been entirely different," the implication being that a faction within the government killed him to scuttle the sale. To sell immediately after Sanaia's killing would have appeared like an act of cowardice and capitulation on Kitsmarishvili's part and would have raised suspicions that Patarkasishvili was somehow behind the murder. The deal was called off, but pressure on the station continued to mount, stronger than before.)

Sitting at a café outside his office in downtown Tbilisi one late October day in 2001, just a few months after Sanaia's death, Kitsmarishvili got a call from his station manager, Nika Tabatadze, from inside the newsroom. "There are five guys here from state security demanding to see our tax returns," he told his boss. "They claim they have a court order." It wouldn't be the first time that the authorities had tried to shut down the muckraking television channel, which by then had a greater audience share than all its competitors combined. Kitsmarishvili calmly suggested they turn their cameras on to "broadcast our conversations live." Within a half hour, a few thousand fans of the channel surrounded the building that housed the station, demanding that the police leave it alone. The officers left, but returned later that afternoon with about thirty Ministry of Interior troops. The crowds of mostly students then grew to tens of thousands and soon surrounded the Parliament. Two days later, the National Security Minister, Vakhtang Kutateladze, the subject of some of Rustavi-2's most damning exposes of high-level corruption and arms dealing, submitted his resignation to President Shevardnadze, who then dismissed his entire cabinet, ending the standoff. Called in to talk with the president, Kitsmarishvili was somewhat taken aback when Shevardnadze asked him, "What should I do? Should I resign?"

"That's not my job. Not my business," responded Kitsmarishvili. "We are independent media. We are not demanding any resignations."

But the demonstrators who surrounded the Parliament and the president's office were thinking of regime change. On everyone's mind was the non-violent revolution that had overthrown President Slobodan Milosevic in Serbia the year before. Like Georgia, an independent media outlet was at the center of the Serbian youth movement that mobilized large crowds against an authoritarian leader. While radio played the key role in Serbia, television was to be the driving force in Georgia. Soon after the Serbian revolution, Georgian opposition leaders, mostly disaffected former protégés of Shevardnadze, including the future president Mikhail Saakashvili and Parliament speaker Zurab Zhvania, traveled to Belgrade to learn about the non-violent civil disobedience techniques perfected by the youth group, Otpur! (Resistance) that had so effectively outmaneuvered the regime there. Two years later, in 2003, leaders of Otpur! went to Tbilisi to instruct a youth group named Kmara! (Enough) that was modeled after them. But the democratic opposition to Shevardnadze at the time did not anticipate any imminent pre-revolutionary period in Georgia as had preceded the overthrow of Milosevic in Serbia, and instead turned its attention to the presidential elections scheduled for 2005.

The government's attempt to shut down Rustavi-2 had backfired. It would be hard to find a clearer example of the power of independent media than this. Rustavi-2 fulfilled the most essential function of the "Fourth Estate"—to be society's watchdog over the government's abuse of authority. Without a free media, governments cannot be held accountable. Democracy depends on it.

The station's success is also a textbook example of the value of media development. US government-funded journalism training programs, station management seminars and technical assistance were what helped build Rustavi-2. But, it should be emphasized, the purpose of media development is to build a robust civil society, never to encourage regime change.

The dilemma for Shevardnadze and other so-called "liberal autocrats" is that they want to allow the growth of civil society and a free market economy, but only so long as it doesn't threaten their hold on power. Georgian political scientist Ghia Nodia put it succinctly: "The assumption of the rulers was that they had to conform to certain norms of liberal democracy . . . To be clear, all this did not mean that the opposition should be allowed to actually displace the ruling elite from power through elections."

Certainly, Shevardnadze needed at least the veneer of democracy to keep Western aid flowing; but given his prodigious role as Gorbachev's Foreign Minister in helping transform Soviet Communism into a democracy and negotiating a peaceful end to the Cold War, Shevardnadze should be given the benefit of the doubt. "When I came back to Georgia in 1992, to the devastated country that lay in shambles after the civil war," he reflected during an interview in 2005 after he had been chased from power, "I had two major aims in mind. First, I wanted to lay the foundation for a market economy, and second, I wanted to make the people of Georgia realize what democracy is." By allowing the existence of independent media, he undoubtedly contributed to the growth of civil society in Georgia. But his tolerance of corruption by his family and government ministers undermined his democratic instincts. Richard Miles, the US ambassador to Georgia during the last years of Shevardnadze's reign, wrote, "Shevardnadze presided over an incredibly corrupt situation. Nonetheless, he was not a tyrant and was not prepared to beat people up and lock them up, although his ruling team did so."

Compared to other post-Soviet states, Georgia under Shevardnadze had a relatively free press. It passed a progressive freedom of information law, decriminalized libel and required that government officials prove malicious intent in any civil libel cases brought against the media. The Committee to Protect Journalists even wrote, "While many of its neighbors in the former Eastern Bloc grew increasingly intolerant of independent journalism, Georgia offered its journalists good news." In the end, though, it all came down to a choice between control and freedom.

As parliamentary elections approached in 2003, Shevardnadze's popularity had plummeted along with the economy and in the face of pervasive corruption; but the opposition was so disunited he felt he had nothing to fear, even though public opinion polls showed his party had the support of less than 15 percent of the population. Kitsmarishvili at

Rustavi-2, however, with his accurate feel for the mood of the people (as reflected in his programming success), sensed a political opportunity. He put up $150,000 of his own money and with additional support from the Soros Foundation, Eurasia, and the British Council, hired the New York company Global Strategy Group to conduct an independent exit poll and a Parallel Vote Tabulation (PVT) that uses sampling of results to give an early prediction of the final vote count, a practice familiar to viewers of network coverage of American elections. Shevardnadze applied what pressure he could to prevent the polling data from being released, including calls to Washington, but the exit polls and the PVT went forward. According to these independent sources, Mikhail Saakashvili's National Movement party came in first with 27 percent of the vote, ahead of the ruling party's bloc in second place with 19 percent. Another three opposition parties garnered a total of 35 percent.

The results alone would not have provoked a revolution, but what did was Rustavi-2's television coverage. As official results streamed in on November 2, 2003, the station ran a constant crawl across the bottom of the screen displaying the government's official figures that showed a win for the ruling party. However, along the right side of the screen exit polls and the parallel vote count were displayed with a decidedly different result. In the center of the screen, live video showed protesters beginning to stream into downtown Tbilisi.

Much to everyone's surprise, on November 4, the second day after the elections, the leading opposition figures joined forces and appeared on Rustavi-2 to call on their followers to gather at the Philharmonic Hall at 5 p.m. A large crowd formed and plans were made for a giant rally the next day at Freedom

Square to be broadcast live on Rustavi-2 and other channels. On November 5, when the Central Election Commission announced that the governing party had won, anger exploded throughout the country. Observers from the Organization of Security and Cooperation in Europe (OSCE) announced the election "did not meet international standards."

A huge crowd massed on Rustaveli Avenue in front of the Parliament and city hall on November 8 and, despite a heavy downpour, continued to grow throughout the night and the next day. Independent television channels provided minute-by-minute coverage of the demonstrations. By the 14th, with the situation spinning out of his control, Shevardnadze told the press "my resignation would be irresponsible. I do not await the fate of either Ceausescu or Milosevic." Committees of civil disobedience began to form all over Georgia. Late on Friday, November 21, the night before a planned massive demonstration, Rustavi-2 broadcast live video of a huge line of cars, a blazing river of headlights, bringing protesters into Tbilisi from all over Georgia. The images stunned the country. Several of the leaders of the opposition pointed to these videos as the tipping point when everyone realized these were not just protests, but the beginning of a revolution.

As tens of thousands of people filled Freedom Square and Rustaveli Avenue, Shevardnadze opened the Parliament, with only the representatives of pro-regime parties in attendance. When he began to speak following the national anthem, opposition leader Mikhail Saakashvili and his supporters suddenly forced their way through locked doors into the chamber carrying red roses (to indicate they were unarmed), yelling at Shevardnadze to resign. Bodyguards hustled the president out of the building while Saakashvili strode to the podium, brazenly downed Shevardnadze's unfinished glass of tea and called on Nino Burjanadze, the speaker of Parliament, to take over as acting president, as specified in the Constitution. Rustavi-2 dubbed the event the "Rose Revolution."

Remarkably, there was no violence in Tbilisi throughout the twenty days of revolutionary protests. Only one window was inadvertently broken as protesters surged into the Parliament. Several commentators credit the non-violent youth group Kmara! for maintaining discipline throughout, as its mentor Otpur! had done in the revolts that toppled Milosevic in Belgrade. But the role of Kmara!, with only three thousand members at the time, and other NGOs may have been romanticized. The real force that mobilized the population and educated them in the tactics of non-violent revolution was Rustavi-2. "The NGOs did have some role in organizing student protests," said President Saakashvili, "but I think this was mostly Rustavi-2's work really. Most of the students who came out on the streets were brought out by Rustavi, not by the NGOs." For days leading up to the seizure of power, Rustavi-2 broadcast and rebroadcast *Bringing Down a Dictator*, a documentary film by Peter Ackerman teaching the tactics of non-violent revolution that had succeeded so brilliantly in Serbia. Georgia may have had the best-educated protesters of any revolution in history, thanks to Ackerman's film and Rustavi-2.

Of course, the lack of violence was also due to the reluctance of the security troops to use force against their fellow Georgians. There's been considerable controversy on this subject. Shevardnadze claimed the opposition knew he "would never fire on them, would never do anything that would cause casualties." But Saakashvili disputed that, saying,

"Shevardnadze really wanted some kind of military clash . . . He gave the order to shoot people. He gave the order to kill me." Whatever the truth, everyone feared the potential for violence. Memories of the 1991-1992 civil war and conflict in the breakaway province of Abkhazia in 1992 and 1993 were still fresh in people's minds. But the non-violent overthrow of Milosevic in Belgrade held out a model for hope. As James Wertsch, a leading scholar on the Georgian revolution concluded, "By the time of the elections on November 2, most Georgians trusted NGOs and the independent media more than the government as a source of information."

The "dictator's dilemma" puts autocrats in a no-win situation: either they stifle democracy and rule by force, or they allow freedom and democracy and accept the will of their people. Halfway measures ultimately don't succeed. When citizens have access to information and the right to speak, but are denied the opportunity to freely elect their leaders, they are primed to revolt.

The Color Revolutions

Georgia's Rose Revolution emboldened activists in other fledgling democracies in the former Soviet Union, sparking popular uprisings that came to be known as "Color Revolutions." At a gathering of heads of state from the Caucasus and Central Asia, in December 2003, shortly after the events in Georgia, President Putin was heard to say, "All the leaders of the CIS (Commonwealth of Independent States) are shitting in their pants."

In Ukraine, an independent cable TV station, Channel 5, played a somewhat similar role in that country's "Orange

Revolution" to Rustavi-2's in Georgia, though it did not have as large an audience or national reach. As elections neared, however, in the fall of 2004, Channel 5's ratings soared from 3 percent to the third mostwatched channel. When President Leonid Kuchma tried to shut the station down just before the balloting for a new president, reporters there went on a hunger strike and the government backed down. By this time the Internet had become a significant source of news in Ukraine. Investigative reports by *Pravda Ukraine*, an online Webbased newspaper started by Georgy Gongadze, a journalist who was kidnapped and decapitated after exposing the corruption of the Kuchma regime, undermined the legitimacy of the government. Onair defections from state television weakened it even further. As the presenter of state-controlled UT1's main morning news program was announcing the Central Electoral Commission's decision to declare Prime Minister Viktor Yanukovych the winner of the country's presidential vote to succeed President Kuchma, Natalya Dmitruk, the woman on television translating the news into sign language, instead signed, "I address all deaf viewers. Yushchenko [the candidate of the democratic opposition to Kuchma and Yanukovych] is our president. Do not believe the Electoral Commission. They are lying." Word of her defiance empowered protesters on the streets.

Ukraine's Orange Revolution succeeded in reversing the fraudulent election results and brought the challenger Viktor Yushchenko to power after a repeat runoff election. Another non-violent Color Revolution followed shortly after Ukraine's in Kyrgyzstan, called the "Tulip Revolution," which overthrew President Askar Akayev. For a few months in the spring of 2004, it seemed like authoritarian regimes were catching a democracy virus that had spread from Georgia's Rose Revolution. By the next year in Lebanon, following the assassination of the opposition leader Rafik Harari, the socalled "Cedar Revolution" brought an end to the Syrian occupation of the country.

The Color Revolutions that spread from Georgia and Ukraine to the Caucasus, Central Asia, and even Lebanon frightened ruling elites in autocratic governments everywhere. The conventional wisdom that newly independent media outlets fueled these popular rebellions prompted a retrenchment of media freedoms. There was little that these undemocratic governments could do to prevent satellite news images of popular revolts from crossing their borders, but they could make it much harder to operate local radio and television stations in their territories once the balance of power shifted back toward authoritarianism. It wasn't until the Internet and the growth of mobile telephony that movements for democratic change again began to emerge, leading to the next wave of democratic uprisings which spread across the Middle East and North Africa. If one country were to be known as the poster child for the dictator's dilemma, it would be Pakistan.

A Media Revolution

I first met Mir Ibrahim Rahman, the young founder and CEO of Pakistan's Geo TV, along with Rustavi-2's Erosi Kitsmarishvili, when they shared the International Broadcasting Excellence Award at the National Association of Broadcasting (NAB) convention in Las Vegas in 2004. Rustavi-2 was recognized for its singular role in support of the non-violent Rose Revolution while Geo won for its ground-breaking "independent, live news coverage and programs based on many important issues never before addressed in the Pakistan media." The Pakistani television station was at the forefront of a veritable media revolution that General Pervez Musharraf, the president of the country, had launched by liberalizing the media, allowing private radio and television stations to operate for the first time in its history.

Kitsmarishvili and Mir, as he is known, are strikingly different personalities, but both are savvy businessmen devoted to freedom and democracy. Named after his grandfather, Mir Khalilur-Rahman, Mir is handsome and intensely focused, with the careful reserve of someone well-bred and accustomed to being around people with power. The elder Mir, who died when his grandson was eight, was a legend in Pakistan. Originally from Kashmir, Mir Khalil-ur-Rahman started an Urdu-language newspaper for Muslims in pre-partition Delhi called the *Jang*, or "War," from which he agitated against Indian Muslims participating in World War II. He delivered copies of the paper himself on a bicycle. With partition, he moved to Karachi and began publishing the *Daily Jang*, which became the country's newspaper of record and grew into the nation's largest media conglomerate.

The younger Mir grew up spending his spare time in the newspaper's office and dreamed of fulfilling his grandfather's wish to start the nation's first private television channel. "Look, if you really want to make an impact on the country, and influence things, and be relevant and try to take the country in the right direction," the elder Mir would tell his grandson, "then we won't be able to do that unless we have television." But there was little prospect of Pakistan's authoritarian government permitting privately owned television in 1996 when Mir went off to Babson College in Boston to study business. Since he was the eldest son and the first in his family to go to college, his parents, aunts, and uncles all accompanied him to orientation. There his father took him aside and said, "Do not come back to Pakistan. Your grandfather left *Jang* for me, not for you."

It was a rude awakening and he and his father did not speak again for several years. After General Musharraf, who took power in a military coup in 1999, announced his intention of privatizing the media in his "Liberation Speech" of 2001, Mir's father called him. "Do you remember what you said to me the night of orientation?" he asked. "You pointed your finger at me and said, 'One day I *will* come back and you will ask me to come back.'" After a long pause, he continued, "Son, I am calling you back. I want you to come back and fulfill your grandfather's dreams and ambitions. He would want you to launch Pakistan's first satellite channel."

There are various theories why Musharraf allowed the first commercial, independent television and radio stations, opening such a Pandora's box of free expression. Partly it was meant to avoid the humiliation he suffered after the Kargil fiasco, a failed military incursion into Indian-administered Kashmir, which he had engineered. With state-run TV telling viewers nothing of the military setbacks, millions of Pakistanis followed events on the burgeoning networks of mom and pop cable stations that pirated the news from Indian satellite channels. Instead of the martial programming on state television, Pakistanis were getting their news unfiltered in real time from their archenemy India.

Musharraf realized he had to do something to stop this, knowing, however, that it was unrealistic to try to reform the bloated state television service. Privately owned commercial media enterprises, on the other hand, could be unleashed to do what private enterprise does best—compete. At a cabinet meeting of 122 people, he was the only one in favor of opening the media. To his credit, Musharraf hoped to be the leader who would modernize Pakistan and make it a part of the globalized economy.

So, in 2002 the government began issuing licenses for private, non-governmental broadcasters, the opportunity Mir and his father had been waiting for. Over the next five years, 130 radio stations and fifty television channels went on the air. In a country of 160 million people (at best only 35 percent literate), the live 24-hour news cycle pioneered by Geo TV turned politics into a national obsession. But in freeing up the media, Musharraf did not take his heel off the political opposition, emasculating independent political parties and forcing their leaders into exile. This inadvertently created a vacuum that the new television channels eagerly filled. As Adnan Rehmat, the journalist and chronicler of Pakistan's media, explained:

> Pakistan's media have articulated well the concerns of the disempowered citizens, seizing this role from the political parties by mobilizing public opinion as well as the intelligentsia—the role that usually political parties do but which have been otherwise rendered impotent by the Orwellian establishment through forced exiles and intimidation of political leaders and rendering the parliament, the only other space where public concerns can be articulated—impotent.

The combination of greater information access and declining options for democratic debate radicalized the population.

In 2007, a surprising hero stepped forward to challenge the regime. Iftikhar Muhammad Chaudhry had been appointed chief justice of the Supreme Court by Musharraf in June 2005, the youngest person to hold that office. He did not look the part of a typical Pakistani leader. He was homely and a poor public speaker; he was not rich, had no public following, and no ethnic power base, nor was he the son of a well-known father. But he did something no other public figure had had the courage to do—stand up to General Musharraf.

It began when Chaudhry acted upon the plea of the mothers of hundreds of nationalist activists, journalists and poets who had "disappeared" while in police custody in the restive province of Baluchistan and reopened an investigation into official misconduct. His next step was to suspend the privatization of the Pakistan Steel Mills, a shady deal that opponents argued would have benefitted Prime Minister Shaukat Aziz. Then, he blocked a controversial housing project tied to various political leaders on environmental grounds. But what finally pushed Musharraf to act against Chaudhry was his demand that the general give up his army uniform in order to run in the upcoming presidential election, as required under the Constitution.

On March 9, 2007, Musharraf ordered Chief Justice Chaudhry to meet him at the Army House in the military garrison of Rawalpindi. There, he informed Chaudhry that he had been suspended and insisted that he immediately resign. Musharraf was in full uniform and brought with him Prime Minister Aziz, the heads of all the military branches and domestic intelligence agencies, and several generals, almost all in uniform. For five hours Musharraf berated him, but the chief justice refused to resign. Pakistan State Television (PTV) recorded the whole inglorious episode and broadcast some visual segments on the evening news, as it did for every meeting Musharraf attended.

When Chaudhry left the meeting, forced to attend a disciplinary hearing of the Judicial Council, he refused to get into a waiting government car and was manhandled by the police, who pulled his hair and pushed him inside the vehicle. A reporter emotionally narrated the events on live television. As Mir later recalled, "I remember watching it. I remember feeling moved. I remember feeling betrayed. I remember feeling like I had been humiliated. I remember watching other people with this intensity as well." As we shall see in later chapters when we observe the Arab Spring, an individual humiliation captured by the media can touch the collective shame of a nation and incite revolutionary rage. The visuals of Chief Justice Chaudhry being berated on PTV as well as being roughly forced into a government car aired endlessly on the ubiquitous cable TV talk shows, igniting mass protests throughout the country.

In the days to follow, television coverage showed Chaudhry under house arrest, his cars removed with forklifts, and all communications cut off to him. For the first time in Pakistan's history, people watched the mounting protests in real time on live television. At least eighty thousand lawyers went on strike. Like most former British colonies, Pakistan reveres the rule of law, even if it does not always practice it, and its jurists command great respect. The unprecedented suspension of a chief justice crossed a red line in the nation's self-respect and provoked a massive protest in support of Chaudhry.

A week after the sacking of the chief justice, a large march by the jurists' movement converging on the Parliament in the capital, Islamabad, turned into a riot when police beat demonstrators and lobbed endless rounds of tear gas into their ranks. Geo TV broadcast the riot live from the rooftop of its studios directly across from the action, despite a government order issued the previous day not to cover any more of the protests. Suddenly, around 4 p.m., the police charged into Geo's building looking for its camera, firing tear gas, ransacking the place and roughing up its staff. Mir was in Karachi at Geo's headquarters and saw what was happening on his monitor. His news director had just left to work for a competitor and Mir had temporarily assumed that position. He instinctively told his bureau chief, "Just turn the camera on. Forget the lawyers' movement. Just show these people coming in."

This attack on the most popular station in Pakistan marked a turning point; what had been a series of street protests became a bona fide media revolt. Recalled Mir, "I saw, on screen, just like the rest of the population, these people quickly entering our offices and throwing computers down and breaking windows and trying to look for that camera. The visual was so powerful that by eight, nine o'clock, Musharraf had to come, live, on our screen to apologize." Pakistan's media had proved the power of its new Fourth Estate.

Like Georgia's Shevardnadze, Pakistan's Musharraf thought of himself as a reformer. He had given birth to the independent media, which was transforming Pakistan into a more modern, open society. These were his children who had turned against him, he must have thought, just as Shevardnadze had felt betrayed by the leaders of the Rose Revolution who had all been his political protégés. But like other "soft dictators," Musharraf had raised expectations for greater freedoms without delivering them. "He gave us this false sense . . . that we are free and things are changing and there was a new Pakistan emerging," Mir reflected. "By 2006, we had the second fastest growing stock market. We had the third fastest growing GDP in the world, after India and China. Things were really looking up . . . I think the mismanagement of expectations and selling of idealism kind of backfired for him."

Even after Musharraf's dramatic apology on television, protests supporting the jurists' movement continued to grow. After Chaudhry was released from house arrest in May 2007, the suspended chief justice drove from Islamabad to Lahore. Hundreds of thousands of people clogged the streets to get a look at him; the 150-mile trip became a twenty-six-hour triumphal celebration with every minute covered live on television. Musharraf was feeling the heat. On July 20, he effectively conceded after the Supreme Court ruled he had fired the chief justice in violation of the Constitution, which vested such authority in the judiciary, not the executive, branch.

Despite this unprecedented victory by Chaudhry and the Court—the first against military authority since the founding of the Republic—the war was not over. A week before presidential elections in October 2007, the Supreme Court again warned Musharraf that it could invalidate the results if he refused to remove his uniform. Musharraf won with 98 percent of the votes in the Senate, Parliament and the four provincial assemblies, all under his control; but on November 3, with the Court expected to nullify his victory, Musharraf declared a state of emergency and suspended the Constitution.

The Dictator's Dilemma

As Rehmat has pointed out, Musharraf's coup was unusual, in that it was not against a sitting government or the military, but against the judiciary and the media in support of an elected president. Sixty judges were arrested and more than thirty television stations banned, including international news channels like CNN and the BBC. Hundreds of journalists were thrown in prison. Musharraf shut all of Geo's channels, including its popular youth and sports channels. Mir's father and Geo's owner, Mir Shakil-ur-Rahman, was taken by the notorious Directorate for Inter-Services Intelligence to a safe house in Islamabad and threatened. Blocked from the airwaves and without advertising revenue, Pakistan's new TV stations were hemorrhaging money. Most of them were allowed back on the air only after signing a secret fourteen-page code of conduct that prohibited them from criticizing the government, but Geo continued to hold out, despite losing half a million dollars a day in lost advertising. Moving its operations to Dubai, it broadcast on a direct-to-home satellite channel. Sales of satellite dishes soared, but Musharraf persuaded the Emir of the United Arab Emirates to force Geo and other Pakistani satellite networks off the air. Along with two other news channels, ARY One World and Aaj TV, Geo switched to broadcasting online. But although emergency rule had accelerated the growth of the Internet and social media in Pakistan, its influence on the ground remained negligible. It wasn't until January 21, 2008, two months after the state of emergency, that Geo finally gave in, signed the code of conduct and was allowed to resume broadcasting.

But the popular forces that Musharraf unleashed when he liberalized the media had, ironically, turned against him. It soon became clear that Musharraf had won the battle, but was losing the war. Pakistan's general election for parliament on

95

February 18, 2008 was seen as a referendum on his presidency. The poll was neither free nor fair; even so, the ruling party received less than a quarter of the vote. Virtually all its senior members, including twenty-two former cabinet ministers, were defeated. The very first act of the new parliament was to repeal the regime's media restrictions and return the law to what it had been prior to emergency rule. By August 7, the Parliament initiated impeachment proceedings against Musharraf and on August 18 he resigned.

Pakistan had changed dramatically after the introduction of independent radio and television in 2002. News and politics were no longer confined to the educated elites. Important events now unfolded in real time, shared across all sectors and classes, creating a national dialogue. Now dozens of television channels competed for audience share, expressing a full array of political points of view. The airwaves became a vibrant public commons, empowering citizens as never before. It will be years, if ever, before the balance of power between the executive and judiciary branches, Parliament, military, and media will be fully resolved. Grinding poverty, religious intolerance, feudal land rights, massive corruption, the war in Afghanistan, and an abysmal education system will continue to threaten the integrity of the state, but the rise of a diverse media puts the country's fate back into the hands of its people.

Both Eduard Shevardnadze and Pervez Musharraf succumbed to the dictator's dilemma. Both wanted to modernize their economies and earn favor with the West by allowing an independent press and private broadcast networks to operate, but neither was willing to tolerate a neutral political playing field. In the end, their people put their faith in the media rather than the government. Corruption and abuse of power exposed by these new media drove both presidents from power.

MYANMAR'S TOP DOWN
REVOLUTION

If more "liberal" dictatorships were unable to control the forces unleashed by independent media, how could a hard line dictatorship ever open its media? Myanmar may offer an intriguing answer. In 2010 the military government of Myanmar surprised the world with its sudden and unexpected moves to introduce democratic reforms across every sector of Burmese society. From the outside, Myanmar, one of the most impenetrable and repressive states on earth, appears to be moving from a hard to a liberal dictatorship in a transition to true democracy. The generals who have ruled Myanmar since 1962 seem confident they can tolerate a peaceful, political opposition that can express itself through the media and periodic elections without sacrificing their authority.

Myanmar has long been considered one of the most authoritarian, closed societies outside of North Korea. It is one of the least developed countries in the world despite abundant natural resources like oil and natural gas. A mere 25 percent of rural homes have electricity. A former British colony, it gained independence in 1948 after the nationalist leader General Aung San succeeded in (tentatively) unifying the majority Burman population with the Karens, Kachin, Shan, and Chin peoples in a loose federation.

General Aung San did not live to see independence, however. He was assassinated on July 19, 1947, along with most of Myanmar's political leadership. Nevertheless, Myanmar experienced a decade of a remarkable experiment in democracy. During these "parliamentary years" of the 1950s, as they are known, there was a flourishing free press with dozens of independent newspapers, including Chinese and Hindi publications. In September 1958, army officers took power from a squabbling parliament and began a crackdown on the media. This "caretaker" government was itself overthrown in a military coup in 1962 when General Ne Win established full military rule. Trade unions and existing political parties were banned and all independent media were suppressed. Only a very few journalists who, for one reason or another, had some access to international news were able to keep alive the dream of someday working in an open media environment.

88ers

One of these, U Thiha Saw, had been a student at Rangoon University (currently Yangon University) in the late 1960s, majoring in nuclear physics when, like many others of his generation, he was caught up in the zeitgeist of radicalism. (In 1989 the military junta changed the name of the capital from Rangoon to Yangon and Burma to Myanmar, provoking debate to this day.) In 1974, while he was teaching and pursuing a second post-graduate degree, Saw was imprisoned for four months in what became known in Myanmar as the "U Thant Crisis." The Burmese-born secretary general of the United Nations, Thant was a severe critic of the military junta. When he died, the authorities planned to give him an ordinary funeral without fanfare, even though he was the most celebrated Burmese citizen in the world. Just before that event, however, Saw and some fellow students stole U Thant's coffin, taking it to a temporary mausoleum at the Rangoon University Students Union, which had been dynamited by General Ne Win during the coup of 1962. When the military stormed the campus and shot and killed some of the students, there were riots in the streets of the capital and martial law was declared.

After his release from prison, Saw kept a low profile, working as a proofreader for two government-run English newspapers before landing a job on the international desk of the state-run News Agency of Myanmar. Although he had to comply with strict censorship rules, the position allowed Saw to read unfiltered international wire service feeds, giving him a unique view of the outside world. A few years later, he became the news agency's editor. Twice a day, he submitted his copy to two military officers and the chief editors of the country's government-run newspapers for their final censorship decisions. In 1986, Saw got the rare chance to leave the country for journalism training in West Berlin.

The year after Saw returned from Berlin, the political situation in Rangoon had become more volatile. In the midst of a worsening economy, General Ne Win announced a demonetization of the nation's currency. With a single decree, all bills in circulation became worthless and new denominations of forty-five and ninety kyat notes were issued—favorite numbers that Ne Win thought lucky because they were divisible by nine. Overnight, most people's savings were wiped out. Students took to the streets and marches quickly escalated into violent confrontations with the military regime.

With no independent media, people tuned to the BBC Burmese Service on shortwave radio to find out what was happening in their own country. At the end of July, in an interview with the BBC's Christopher Gunness, an unnamed student called for nationwide demonstrations on August 8, 1988 (8-8-88), an auspicious date of great import in Burmese culture. At exactly 8:08 a.m. on the eighth, dockworkers went on strike and people poured into the streets of Rangoon.

For five days, soldiers opened fire on student demonstrators, killing three thousand people in protests that raged across the country. When the shooting finally stopped, revolutionary committees formed in every town in Myanmar to try to maintain order in the face of an almost complete breakdown of government services. With the sudden thaw in tensions, Saw organized a takeover of the six leading papers in the capital—all government owned—and together with the News Agency of Myanmar formed a "boycott committee" to publish a joint daily newspaper. When the new paper was first distributed, people thought it was another government publication and began burning piles of them, until they realized there were pictures of demonstrators on the front page. This was uncensored news! It seemed incomprehensible that there could be an independent paper. Dozens of other newspapers then appeared overnight. For twentyfive days, Myanmar had a free press. I asked Saw if he expected to get arrested each day. "No," he said, "we were expecting we would get killed."

Students called for a nationwide strike on August 26 and half a million people gathered to hear Aung San Suu Kyi, the daughter of Myanmar's independence leader, speak for the first time. "The Lady," as she is now called, electrified the crowd. But despite overwhelming popular opposition to the military, the protesters were unable to form an interim government, and on September 18, 1988, the military staged another coup and took back control of the country. On July 20, 1990, Aung San Suu Kyi was placed under house arrest and many of the leaders of her newly formed party, the National League for Democracy (NLD), were sent to prison. Even with this wholesale harassment, voting on Election Day was relatively free and the NLD scored an overwhelming victory, taking 392 of the 485 parliamentary seats, including all 59 seats in the capital. But the Parliament was never allowed to convene and the democracy movement was crushed.

The democracy protests of 1988 and the arrests and killings of thousands of demonstrators became the defining narrative of Burmese political life up to today.

Media Underground

Most of the student leaders and young journalists who weren't arrested fled the country. U Thiha Saw, however, decided to stay. Surprisingly, he was not arrested, but was forced to retire from the news agency. Two years after the coup, he began publishing a monthly business magazine called *Myanma Dana (Prosperity)*, the first of its kind, but he was arrested and jailed for seventy-five days when he printed a picture of The Lady in full color. Although nongovernmental periodicals were permitted, they were not allowed to cover any news stories. Saw continued with his business monthly and his circulation increased substantially.

With strict censorship and a ruthless military dictatorship, editors of independent publications like Saw were not able to speak freely; instead, they relied on subtle allegory. For example, on the birthday of Min Ko Naing, one of the most prominent student leaders of the '88 protests, William Chen, editor of *Kumudra* and *The Modern Weekly*, ran a photo of an oil painting by the student's father, a renowned artist, that included a figure speaking at a microphone that might have represented the son. When I asked Chen what article he was most proud of during this time, he mentioned, with a wry smile, his series on Myanmar's electricity shortage called "People Living in the Dark." But these obtuse criticisms were no substitute for free and independent media.

The only real news of what was happening inside Myanmar came from journalists operating underground, risking arrest and torture. Following the bloody crackdown of 1988, hundreds of students fled Rangoon to join the numerous ethnic armies (Shan, Mon, Karen, Kachin and others) in their jungle bases in border areas where they had been fighting a succession of governments for decades. In due course the student fighters and activists filtered illegally across the border to Thailand. After the junta arrested Aung San Suu Kyi and nullified the results of the 1990 election, a new wave of NLD supporters and elected parliamentarians joined the swell of disaffected exiles on the Thai border, forming a thriving activist community that served as a focal point for Western funding for Burma's struggle for democracy.

As the military regime tightened its grip on the media inside Myanmar after its drubbing in the polls, exiles provided information on what was happening within the country. Hundreds of young reporters who had crossed illegally into Thailand, Bangladesh, and India received extensive training at a school for exiled Burmese journalists just across the border in

Chiang Mai, Thailand. A handful of dissident exile media groups produced newspapers and activist literature that combined fact, rumor, and opinion gleaned from migrant workers, monks, soldiers, tea-shop owners, and other informants inside the country with news from the BBC and other international broadcasters. Thousands of copies of these publications were smuggled at great risk back across the border in an attempt to keep the people of Myanmar informed about events in their own country. Anyone found reading one of these prohibited publications was automatically sentenced to seven years in jail. For almost two decades, Myanmar remained in virtual media darkness, but the few underground media outlets and memories of the short-lived struggles of the 8-8-88 democracy movement kept some hope of freedom alive.

As new video and digital technologies became available, groups of journalists risked their lives by secretly filming evidence of human rights abuses by the army in the ethnic state conflict zones. These underground videographers smuggled their tapes to colleagues in Thailand who sent them to international news agencies and the Democratic Voice of Burma, an expatriate Burmese language satellite television channel uplinked from Oslo, Norway, that has been broadcasting into Myanmar since 2005. Few people in Myanmar have access to satellite dishes, but through word of mouth, news of what had been broadcast reached the intellectual community, the remnants of the National League for Democracy, and eventually other segments of the population. Still, most of Myanmar's people had little, if any, idea of what was happening outside their village or town.

The work of these video journalists gained international attention with the release of *Burma VJ: Reporting from a Closed Country*, a remarkable film by Anders Ostergaard, a Danish documentary filmmaker. Using a *cinema verite* style, the film's narrator, "Joshua," a clandestine reporter for the Democratic Voice of Myanmar, secretly shoots underground video of demonstrators bravely confronting the military regime. There is archival footage of the mass student revolts in 1988 and Aung San Suu Kyi's historic speech, followed by shots of wounded and dead protesters. With the incessant rain and dirge-like soundtrack, the film is infused with a sense of hopelessness. "These people were so brave," intones the reporter, "but sometimes I feel they died for nothing. There is nothing left from '88. It's as if everything has been forgotten."

The film documents the September 2007 events in the capital. Anger spreads through the crowd as the police violently drag protesters into vans. As demonstrations continue, groups of red-robed monks take to the streets in silent protest. They protect Joshua and other Democratic Voice of Myanmar journalists and place them in the front of their march. The monks' strength and dignity pose a moral force confronting the helmeted soldiers amassed against them behind metal shields, barbed wire, and machine guns. The monks' ranks swell into the thousands and then tens of thousands, as the people join in behind them. From every balcony people are applauding. The tension rises sharply. Will the army fire at the monks or abandon their weapons and join the people? It is always risky to deploy armed force against non-violent protesters, especially in a country like Myanmar where monks are held in such reverence. The regime cannot be sure that the military will follow its orders. Plus, there are as many monks—four hundred thousand of them—as there are soldiers.

The monks sit down in the streets before the soldiers and pray. Then, with brutal determination, the army moves forward and begins to beat and arrest them. Tear gas fills the air and shots are fired. As the film ends, the revolution for democracy is crushed by the armed forces and despair once again descends on Myanmar like a monsoon.

After forty years of harsh dictatorship and the worst economic performance of any country in the region, Myanmar appeared on the verge of revolution. But the "Saffron Revolution," named after the red robes of the monks, ended in defeat.

Myanmar's generals went to great lengths to keep information about the revolt from the outside world, but reporters like Joshua and the many citizen journalists trained by Western NGOs in Thailand managed to get out an array of photos and videos of the rebellion. Secretly coordinated by a small group called the Myanmar Bloggers Society (which worked out of the offices of a commercial firm teaching basic IT skills in Yangon), these brave journalists enabled the story of the Saffron Revolution to reach the international media, where it dominated the news for weeks. It was no surprise that the crackdown on dissent brought global condemnation. In response, the junta shut down Internet access and disabled international mobile phone connections, even though less than half of 1 percent of Myanmar's forty-eight million people had online or mobile access.

In a country as opaque as Myanmar, it is impossible to know how the Saffron Revolution affected decision-making inside the regime. The anger and dissatisfaction of the people were obvious and the attacks on the monks and the desecration of their monasteries would not easily be forgotten.

In February 2008, five months after the protests ended, the regime put forth a new constitution that had been in the works for fifteen years. It allowed limited civilian rule and announced a national referendum for May. Twenty-five percent of the seats were reserved for the military and the president was required to have a military background. There were other provisions which guaranteed continued military rule, but the Constitution seemed to offer at least a bare minimum of renewed political activity. Anyone campaigning for a "no" vote in the referendum, however, could be imprisoned for three years and the government forbade the media from covering the vote-no campaign.

On May 2, just before the polling took place, Cyclone Nargis battered the Irrawaddy Delta with 160-kilometer per hour winds, passing close by the former capital, Yangon. (In March 2006, the military government relocated the capital to Naypyidaw.) One hundred thirty thousand people were killed. At first, the regime turned down all international help, but finally relented and permitted foreign aid workers into the country. Still, the junta refused to postpone the referendum, even in the midst of the worst disaster in the country's history.

Most political commentators considered the new constitution a complete sham. But in 2009, there were hints that the military junta was prepared to take some real steps toward democratic reform, with the scheduling of a general election for November 2010. Aung San Suu Kyi was permitted to meet with foreign dignitaries and officials from her party, but the NLD opted not to participate in the election.

On November 13, 2010, just days after the polls closed, in a carefully orchestrated play for international approval, the junta released the Nobel laureate from house arrest where she had been detained for fifteen of the past twenty-one years. At the end of March 2011, a former general, Thein Sein, was sworn in as Myanmar's first non-interim civilian president in almost fifty years, and over the months that followed hundreds of political prisoners were released. The right to unionize was legalized in principle and opposition political parties were allowed to compete in future elections. Aung San Suu Kyi declared that the country was "on the verge of a breakthrough to democracy" and agreed to participate in elections scheduled for April 2012.

There are many theories as to why one of the world's worst dictatorships would voluntarily embark on a path of democratic reforms. The crushing of the monks' rebellion may have created dissention within the military leadership. The Arab Spring may have frightened them. According to a cable released by WikiLeaks, General Than Shwe, the military dictator, told a group of visitors that he "had a strong desire not to appear before an international tribunal." Perhaps it was simply a move to avoid a loss of face and allow Myanmar to take its turn in 2014 as chair of the Association of Southeast Asian Nations (ASEAN). That the country was falling behind some of its most undeveloped neighbors like Cambodia and Laos was deeply embarrassing and the generals may have concluded they needed democratic reforms to attract foreign investment. U Thiha Saw and many other Myanmar watchers think the primary reason was a fear of China's influence in the country and a perceived need to engage the United States as a counterweight to its large and powerful neighbor to the east. Indeed, the cancellation of the $3.6 billion Myitsone Dam, financed by the Chinese to provide electricity to Yunnan Province, signaled a major change in Myanmar's foreign policy and a turn to the West.

As the full scope of Myanmar's reforms played out, however—from the release of Aung San Sui Kyi to the passage of a direct foreign investment act—it seemed increasingly plausible that the military regime had been planning this unprecedented liberalization since at least 1992 when it first ordered a National Convention, or Constituent Assembly, to draft a new constitution, as its new president Thein Sein reportedly told President Obama. The breadth of the reforms in virtually every sector of Myanmar's political, economic, and social life suggests this is so. Whatever the reasons for the military regime's dramatic about-face, Myanmar's political reforms—occurring without the pressure of internal rebellion or outside force—are unprecedented and exceptional.

The question now is how the "dictator's dilemma" will play out in the months and years ahead. Having experienced periods of political reform in its past, each followed by renewed repression—the "parliamentary period" following independence, the elections of 1990 that were swept by the NLD, a short-lived release of Aung San Suu Kyi in 1995—the Burmese are naturally skeptical. After all, the new Constitution guarantees the military will have indefinite control over the constitutional process. Because only a handful of seats were contested in the 2012 elections, the governing party, the Union Solidarity and Development Party (USDP), together with the military members of Parliament, presumably would have a super majority until at least 2015 when the next general election is scheduled.

But the generals may have badly underestimated the people's desire for democracy. When the constitutional court ruled that the parliament did not have the power to summon ministers to testify before it, arguing that it was subordinate to the administration, the government party voted with the opposition to impeach the justices, a united front of all the civilian parties. Only the military MPs voted to support the judges. It was a stunning loss for the military regime, signaling that the generals no longer had the absolute political control they had once assumed. Aung San Suu Kyi secretly rushed to see president Sein to assure him that this was not the first step in a revolt that would next try to impeach him. That The Lady, the regime's prisoner for so many years, would need to reassure the president was a sign of the power of democratic reforms that had been released along with her.

The newly assertive independence of the legislature, together with pending reforms of the banking sector and openings for direct foreign investment, foretell dramatic changes in Myanmar's economic and political life, but the greatest challenge remains the reconciliation of the country's 135 ethnic minorities into the body politic. Battling for their independence for decades, non-Burman ethnic and linguistic groups comprise a third of Myanmar's population and occupy half its territory. While moves have been made to achieve ceasefires with armed groups since Thein Sein assumed the presidency, ethnic strife including endemic bad feeling between Buddhists and Muslims across the country threatens the viability of the reforms and could even bring down the government itself. Providing a voice and access to information for these long-oppressed and marginalized minorities will be essential to any democratic transformation in the country.

The litmus test of democratic reforms will be the regime's commitment to a free and open media. On August 20, 2012, the Ministry of Information summoned journalists for an important announcement. It was a Monday, "censorship day" for Nyein Nyein Naing, a thirty-year-old executive editor of 7 Day News, the largest independent news weekly in the country (there were no dailies). She was on her way to the censorship office, housed in a former Japanese torture chamber, with a copy of the next week's paper for its review when she got word of the pending announcement. Crammed into the Ministry's office with journalists from the more than fifty weekly journals, she was stunned when the deputy minister proclaimed that henceforth there would be no pre-publication censorship. Holding up a raft of galleys in her hands, she asked, innocently, "Does that mean I don't have to hand these in?" Told "yes," she returned to her newsroom and, together with her co-executive editor Ahr Mahn, decided to test the limits of this new press freedom. They replaced their lead story with another on the fighting in Kachin State, including photos of refugees fleeing to China. Prior to this announcement, the story unquestionably would have been censored, the paper suspended and its editors possibly jailed. But nothing happened. Forty years and twenty days of press censorship appeared to have come to an end.

Years before, Ahr Mahn and Nyein Nyein Naing first met at a journalism training program in the home of a Yangon diplomat. Ahr Mahn, whose parents are farmers, still looks, inexplicably, like a fifteen-year-old, with the unbridled enthusiasm of a young crusader. Nyein Nyein has a more serious demeanor. Her father had been an NLD MP in 1990 and was jailed after the elections. Nyein Nyein and Ahr Mahn are bold and determined. They joined *7 Day News* at its inception in 2002 as junior reporters and rose to be the paper's joint editors. In the year before the August 20 announcement, *7 Day News* grew from weekly sales of 80,000 to 150,000 papers, capturing 34 percent of the market. Like editors at every other weekly, they dreamed of starting a daily newspaper and began experimenting with a daily news feed on their Facebook page, the only uncensored space at that time in Myanmar's fledgling media. By August 2012, they had 93,000 followers. Together with six other journalists, they petitioned president Sein for licenses to launch the country's first daily newspapers.

The younger generation of journalists, including Ahr Mahn and Nyein Nyein, are decidedly more optimistic than the "88ers," who are more sober and cautious. Thiha Saw, part of this older generation, ran a piece in *Myanma Dana* about farmers protesting land seizures, then nervously waited up all night for the dreaded knock at the door from the security forces, which never came. When I asked Ahr Mahn what were the new red lines, he shrugged his shoulders and said, "There are none." The younger reporters broke off from the old Myanmar Writers and Journalists Association to form their own press association, the Myanmar Journalists Network, but both groups have worked together on a new press council, of which the minister of information asked to come up with a "zero draft" for new media laws that the Ministry will likely publish and claim as its own.

Another noteworthy event, also in August 2012, was a presidential news conference, the first ever held in the country. Ahr Mahn was selected to ask President Thein Sein the first question. "Do you plan to tell parliament how much you are spending on the Kachin conflict?" he asked, a subject that was inconceivable to broach just weeks before. The press conference was carried live on SkyNet, a new direct-to-home satellite television broadcaster that produces what is essentially Myanmar's first independent television news program, *Up To Date*. The government allowed it to broadcast the conference, but required that it wait two hours before transmitting the question and answer period, which it did without any interference.

SkyNet carries sixty-eight channels, including Voice of America and the BBC World Service. Subscription costs dropped to $150 a year, but that remains out of reach for most Burmese. However, SkyNet plans to launch a free-to-air terrestrial channel that could profoundly expand Myanmar's media space. As occurred in both Georgia and Pakistan, a national independent news channel can develop a loyal following that an authoritarian regime suppresses at its peril.

Sai Zom Pha, SkyNet's young, business savvy general manager, comes from the same mold as Georgia's Erosi Kitsmarishvili and Pakistan's Mir Ibrahim Rahman—smart, determined, and strategic. He has to carefully navigate around the older, more conservative cadre among SkyNet's one thousand employees, as well as the government itself. But he has big plans. When I recounted the story of how Rustavi-2 and Geo TV turned their cameras on live when their governments tried to shut them down, his face lit up with the excitement of someone who just learned of a forbidden pleasure.

Myanmar is like Rip Van Winkle, waking from forty years of deep sleep. The changes are coming so fast as to be disorienting. Writing in the *New Yorker*, Evan Osnos described the mood in the country as "not so much joy as vertigo." In relaying his interview of one of the hundreds of "prisoners of conscience" who emerged from confinement anxious to try the Internet, Osnos wrote, it "feels like the whole country is stepping out of jail." Uncensored daily newspapers and independent television and radio stations will give the average Burmese greater access to information than anyone could have predicted. In a country with fewer cell phones than North

Korea, telecom liberalization will vastly expand access to the Internet and bring exponentially greater connectivity to the population. The price of a SIM card in 2010 was $2,000. Two years later the price had dropped to $200. Four new telecoms will compete with the former government monopoly, further lowering prices. President Thein Sein told his countrymen, "In my heart, I want everyone to have connectivity for free." A population that has lived in almost total information darkness will now have a voice.

Much depends on President Thein Sein. It is utterly perplexing how a former general in a repressive military regime could become the advocate for such wholesale political change. He was, after all, the prime minister when the monks' rebellion was brutally crushed. But he has a reputation for not being corrupt, contrary to his predecessor, General Than Shwe. The way out of the paradox of the "dictator's dilemma" is for a leader to embrace democratic change and be prepared to surrender power. Both Georgia's Shevardnadze and Pakistan's Musharraf were seen as corrupt, and while both should get credit for freeing their media, neither would submit to the will of the people.

The verdict is still out on President Thein Sein and his government until the results of the 2015 general election and the army's reaction to it are known. Many who have suffered under Myanmar's ugly dictatorship remain skeptical about the ultimate outcome of the reforms, but there is also a grudging respect for the new president, with many believing he represents Myanmar's best hope for change. One prominent critic of the former military regime, alluding to the fact that the president requires a pacemaker, told me "how frightening it is that so much depends on a little box in that man's chest."

The people who should be most skeptical of the president's motives are the prisoners of conscience and their families, yet their attitude is encouraging. An activist friend described what happened when the first wave of political prisoners was released in September 2012. Instead of chastising their loved ones' captors, the waiting families raised their fists in the air and shouted, "Long live the president!"

PART II

THE GIFT OF
PROMETHEUS

THE USES AND
ABUSES OF MEDIA

Strapped to the mesh liners inside a C-130 like another box of cargo, we flew in a corkscrew pattern down to the Sarajevo airport to avoid any possible anti-aircraft flak, as unlikely as that might be. The airport was under the control of UNPROFOR, the United Nations Protection Force for the Former Yugoslavia, and agreements to end the fighting, the Dayton Accords, had been signed just weeks earlier. Along the strip known as "Snipers' Alley," from the airport into the old city center, were remnants of twisted and burned out cars and trucks. None of the buildings downtown had been spared. The stone and concrete facades bore gaping wounds and were pockmarked with bullet holes. When I arrived at the Internews office, close by the famed National Library of Bosnia and Herzegovina that had been relentlessly bombed into oblivion by gunners on the hills surrounding the city, it was already 6 p.m. It was time for the staff to break out the *slivovitz*, a plum brandy that had helped sustain survivors of the longest siege of a capital city in modern warfare, the elegant host of the Winter Olympics just a decade before. Our office turned into a kind of post-apocalyptic salon each evening.

Precisely at six, Madame Olga walked in, impeccably coiffed and dressed, an eighty-year-old widow who lived in an eighthfloor apartment whose façade had been blown off one day while she lunched at her dining room table. Haris Pasovic, the much lionized playwright and film director who somehow kept the city's film festival alive throughout the siege, stopped by as he always did, along with a score of other artists and intellectuals. One met the most amazing people in Sarajevo, either completely crazy or egoless, having overcome the persistent madness of the war.

The next day Amir Ibrovic, our project director, took me on a tour of the front-line trenches he had helped defend, carefully avoiding the landmines, and then drove us up to his former apartment, which he was about to see for the first time since his family was chased away by Serb paramilitary forces. The apartment had been vandalized and defiled. Next to a window looking down upon the city center were spent shell casings and tacked to the windowsill were photos of Ibrovic's family—apparently, he believed, so that his former neighbors-turned-militiamen could target them through their rifle scopes. Ibrovic proudly lifted his shirt to show me the scar from the bullet that had struck him just over his heart.

A Rip Tide of Democracy

The war in the former Yugoslavia was a counterpoint to the jubilation that followed the liberation of other East European Communist states, raining on the parade of the "end of history" optimism that infected the triumphant Western allies. NATO, which prided itself for staring down the massive military might of the Warsaw Pact, proved inept and cowardly in the face of the first genocide since World War II. The United States, refusing to be the policeman of the world, insisted that

Yugoslavia, sitting in the very heart of Europe, was a European problem. But Europe wouldn't act.

If Vietnam was the first war to be televised, the Balkan conflict was the first war truly driven by television. The rise to power by the Serbian president Slobodan Milosevic was built on a strategy to control Yugoslavia's mass media; and once in control, he used it to foment ethnic hatred and war. Media were at the center of the political intrigues that tore apart the federal republic, incited ultranationalism, and provoked ethnic cleansing. In the end it was an alternative radio station, around which a democratic opposition rallied, that eventually forced Milosevic from power.

A Media Creation

Milosevic was born in 1941 and grew up in a highly dysfunctional family—his mentally ill father used a shotgun to put a bullet in his head and his mother hanged herself from a light fixture—but his fortunes changed when he married his childhood sweetheart, Mirjana Markovic. "Mira," as she was known, came from a high-ranking Communist family. Her aunt had been the private secretary and mistress of Josip Tito, Yugoslavia's president. Ambitious and fiercely authoritarian, Mira worked behind the scenes to advance her husband's career. He got his start as a low-level Communist Party apparatchik employed by the Belgrade city government propaganda office, where he first caught the attention of some of the country's top media executives.

According to Slavoljub Djukic, one of the most respected journalists in Yugoslavia and author of a four-volume biography of Milosevic and his wife, Mira conspired with a small group of powerful media bosses to propel her husband to the presidency of Serbia and promote their radical Serb ideology. Dusan Mitevic and Radomir Vico, directors of Radio Television of Serbia, Zivorad Minovic, editor-in-chief of *Politika*, the largest daily newspaper, and Slobodan Jovanovic, editor of *Politika Ekspres,* met regularly with Milosevic's wife to plot his ascension and sideline his more moderate opponents. As Kemal Kurspahic, a celebrated journalist and author, wrote in *Prime Time Crime*, "It is conventional wisdom among analysts of the Milosevic era that the first thing he did after coming to power was to establish control of the media. The fact is, however, that the media actually gave birth to Milosevic."

Beginning in May 1987, this small group launched a series of coordinated attacks in *Politika*, the newspaper of record and the oldest in the Balkans, against the minister of culture that escalated into a battle between Milosevic's hard-line nationalist faction and moderates, led by Ivan Stambolic, the Serbian president. Stambolic, Milosevic's mentor and best man at his wedding, had assiduously promoted his protégé up the Party ranks. With his wife's prodding, however, Milosevic turned on him. In a dramatic showdown at a Central Party Committee meeting on September 23-24 (a raucous thirty-hour gathering broadcast for the first time live on television), Milosevic emerged victorious, forcing Stambolic to resign. (Years later, Milosevic would be charged with ordering the kidnapping and murder of his former friend.)

Immediately following their triumph, the Milosevic "family," as they were known, began purging thousands of workers at Belgrade TV, the main television channel under Radio Television of Serbia, and turned *Politika* into a mouthpiece of virulent Serb nationalism. With just four key media allies,

Milosevic was able to control 90 percent of the information available to the Serb population.

In Search of a Greater Serbia

Yugoslavia was a strong federal state under Tito's relatively benign authoritarianism. A mosaic of separate nationalities, the country was firmly unified under the leadership of the Communist Party and the national army. Unlike its sister East European Communists in states that had been occupied by the Soviets, Yugoslavians enjoyed considerably greater freedom, especially to travel to the West. But after Tito's death in 1980, nationalist movements began to erode the country's unity. With no chosen successor to Tito, the federal presidency was shared among representatives of Serbia, Croatia, Bosnia, and the other republics.

Kosovo, with 90 percent of its population Albanian, became an autonomous province under the 1974 Yugoslavian Constitution. But Kosovo remained the historic seat of Serb identity, the emotional heart of the Serbian nation. As the new president of Serbia and with his control of the mass media, Milosevic exploited ancient ingrained feelings of Serbian persecution to launch a muscular movement to unite minority Serb populations outside Serbia proper into a "Greater Serbia." The campaign would start in Kosovo.

In April 1987, a meeting called by minority Serb nationalists in Kosovo Polje—the "Field of Blackbirds," site of an historic battle when Ottoman Turk armies defeated the Serbs— drew fifteen thousand angry protesters demanding an end to Kosovo's special status as an autonomous province. Milosevic was sent by the Belgrade party to try to calm passions. But the organizers had planned to provoke a confrontation with the police. Before he left for the event, Milosevic's wife called Dusan Mitevic, himself a Serb from Kosovo, who arranged to provide extensive television coverage of the event. As the police responded to a hail of stones from the protesters, Milosevic strode to the podium and, with the cameras rolling, defiantly told the crowd, "No one is allowed to beat you!" It was an iconic, if largely staged, moment that was replayed endlessly on Serbian TV. With the collaboration of the media, Milosevic had turned himself into the hero who would defend the Serb nation.

The media campaign in Kosovo became a model for other televised mass rallies held to incite a resurgent Serb nationalism in areas where they formed a minority. Thousands of Serb militants were trucked to successive demonstrations, with the media dutifully following along. The language was always one of victimization—by Kosovar "Turks," Croatian Ustashi fascists, Slovenes, and others. Millions turned out for these so-called "Meetings of Truth" throughout Serbia, Yugoslavia's largest republic, to support the "besieged Serb minority" in Kosovo. The exploitation of historic Serb grievances and feelings of victimization reached an apotheosis in the summer of 1990 when the bones of Serbs killed by the Naziinstalled Croatian Ustasha regime fifty years before were excavated, carried from village to village and then reburied by Orthodox priests in ceremonies extensively covered by Milosevic-controlled media.

Ever the opportunist, Milosevic had hitched his wagon to the cause of Serb nationalism and was willing to break up the federal government Tito had constructed to achieve his plans for a Greater Serbia. Milosevic switched his base of power from the national Yugoslavian Socialist Party (formerly the

Communist Party) to the Serb presidency, thereby sidelining and even scapegoating the Communist Party, the unspoken target for what he called his "Anti-Bureaucratic Revolution." Nationalism replaced Communism. In Novi Sad, the capital of Vojvodina, Serbia's other autonomous province, thousands of protesters, many drunk, jeered the local Communist Party leadership and, as they had in Kosovo, pelted the police with stones. With Belgrade TV providing live coverage, the protesters threw jars of yogurt at the building in what became known as "The Yogurt Revolution" of October 1988.

Trapped inside, the terrified Vojvodina party leaders called Milosevic on the phone to beg the army to intervene. Sitting with Dusan Mitevic in his office at Belgrade TV, Milosevic watched the drama unfold on television. He then told the beleaguered officials, "Submit your resignations. If you resign, I'll save you." They did. Two days later, Montenegro was next. Accusing the Montenegrin party leadership of failing to heed the national will, Milosevic's rowdy followers succeeded in chasing the Montenegrin regime from power. Milosevic's reach now extended beyond the territory of Serbia. For the other republics, Milosevic's drive for a Greater Serbia threatened the very existence of Yugoslavia.

By the summer of 1990, spurred by the independence movements in the rest of East Europe, demands for freedom and democratization competed with the forces of resurgent nationalism. Unlike in the other East European Communist states, however, where movements for national independence and democracy banded together to resist foreign occupation, those agitating on behalf of Yugoslavia's nationalist identities splintered along ethnic lines.

In June, when Serbia held a referendum on a new constitution and whether to become a democratic state, seventy thousand people demonstrated in Belgrade in support of multiparty elections. But when marchers rallied in front of state TV, police savagely beat them. The referendum passed, but Milosevic's powers as Serbia's president actually increased under the new constitution. With all the major media firmly supporting him, Milosevic had no trouble winning the presidential election in December, getting more than 65 percent of the vote.

Neighboring Croatia had its own multiparty elections seven months earlier, ousting the Communists and bringing to power the ultranationalist Franjo Tudjman and the HDZ (Hrvatska Demokratska Zajednica), his anti-Communist Croatian Democratic Union party. Croatia under the HDZ was every bit as chauvinist as Milosevic's Serbia. Its flag and symbols were taken from the World War II Croatian fascist regime, the Ustase Independent State of Croatia. The Ustase had brutalized Serbs during the war and exterminated at least fifty thousand Serb partisans at the infamous Jasenovac concentration camp. The HDZ's victory raised the fear that Tudjman would resurrect the old Ustase regime, especially threatening the Serb minority living in Croatia's Krajina region. His dream of a Greater Croatia was destined to clash with Milosevic's one of a Greater Serbia.

A Language of War

The media, once controlled by the Communists, were now directed by the nationalists, giving Serbia's leaders fresh legitimacy. The war eventually to be fought with guns was first being waged in the media. Belgrade TV produced its own nationalist coverage of Kosovo pre-empting TV Pristina,

Kosovo's provincial channel, and causing Croatia and Bosnia to pull out of the federal TV exchange that in previous years had shared programming without incidents. As noted by Mark Thompson, the veteran observer of media in the Balkans, the new media language became "a language of menacing ultimatums, of infinite self-pity, of immense accusations backed by no evidence or investigation; of conspiracy mongering, paranoia, and brazen incitement to violence. It was, in fact, a language of war before war was even conceivable in Yugoslavia."

As tensions built between Serbia and the other Yugoslav republics, opposition to Milosevic's Greater Serbia strategy and his stifling of press freedoms began to mount in Belgrade. The fever of democratic revolutions that had become a contagion throughout the East European Communist bloc raised hopes, as earlier mentioned, and encouraged activists in Yugoslavia as well. The cultural restrictions of Tito's Yugoslavia dissolved and the youth of Belgrade partied like never before. Wrote the journalist Matthew Collin:

> *Change was coming but exactly what kind of change, no one could quite predict. For those who weren't looking over their shoulders, the summer of 1989 was the greatest party Belgrade had ever seen. But while the city's youth reveled in their new-found freedoms, they displayed distinct undertones of suppressed hysteria—as if this might be the last chance to live like this, and so those pleasures must be enjoyed as intensely as possible, before they disappeared forever.*

In May 1989, just as Milosevic's purges of state media went into high gear, Belgrade's Communist youth organization decided to create an experimental, independent radio station called Youth Radio B92, using a studio downtown and an ancient low-powered transmitter on a hill just outside of the capital. Its founding director was twenty-seven-year-old Veran Matic, who had been running a cult student radio show, *Rhythm of the Heart,* that played indie rock and pushed the boundaries of free speech. B92 became the voice of the democratic opposition to Milosevic. Offering one of the few alternatives to the propagandistic news reports carried by Milosevic-controlled state media, B92's mixture of culture, news and politics was a perpetual provocation. "To be normal meant to be subversive," said Matic. Part of a wave of radical "free radio" stations that arose in Europe and the US, B92 personified the activist slogan of one of the most famous of these, Radio Alice in Italy: "Information is not just the repetition or the display of what is going on in reality, but it is a means of transforming reality."

The decisive moment when war became inevitable was on March 9, 1991 during a large march for press freedom in Belgrade. Protesters demanded an end to government control of the media and the resignation of Dusan Mitevic, the head of Belgrade Television who had helped engineer Milosevic's rise to power. Forty thousand demonstrators faced scores of riot police who pounded them with water cannons and tear gas, but the protesters held their ground and chased the police out of the city center. Matic narrated the action as it unfolded in Republic Square below B92's studio. For a few hours it seemed the demonstrators had won.

Milosevic, at a military compound outside the city, telephoned Borisav Jovic, president of Yugoslavia and commander-in-chief of the army, and demanded he send in the tanks. As the Yugoslav army, once the guardian of national unity, was invading its own capital, riot police kicked in the doors of B92 and ordered it off the air. The next night, however, a thousand students broke through the police cordon and again occupied the city center. A hundred thousand protesters poured in and, braving freezing temperatures, camped out for a week singing endless rounds of "Give Peace a Chance."

Milosevic, shaken by the strength of the demonstrations, invited representatives of the opposition to meet with him. They insisted he fire Mitevic and the interior minister. On March 13, hoping to clear the demonstrators from the streets, Milosevic appeared to give in to the protesters' demands. But once the protesters had left, he replaced Mitevic with another hardliner at Belgrade television and pressed the military to take control of the city. With tanks entering the capital, the handwriting was on the wall. The forces of separation were far stronger than any for a unified Yugoslavia. Milosevic secretly met with Franjo Tudjman, the Croatian leader, in Karadjordjevo, Tito's favorite villa, and discussed how they might carve up the nation between them.

A Media War

Serbian media under Milosevic made no attempt to report the news accurately. For example, when Serb paramilitary forces seized a Croat police station in the town of Pakrac and Tudjman's troops retook the town, Serb newspapers and television endlessly reported that eleven Serbs had been killed, including an Orthodox priest, a story that was totally fabricated. But true or not, the news inflamed passions in the capital and the federal army sent in tanks to separate the two sides, intervening in Croatia for the first time. Now there was no turning back.

As the war drums beat in Croatia, Serb nationalists in Bosnia prepared to fight as well. Before seizing territory, however, they first moved to expropriate the airwaves. On August 1, the "War of the Transmitters" began when Serb paramilitary forces in Bosnia took over a television transmitter on Kozara Mountain. Soon after, they seized others in the Bosnian towns of Pljesevica, Doboj, Trovrh, Velez, and Vlasic. Fear spread throughout these areas outside Sarajevo with large Muslim populations; the inhabitants felt threatened and cut off from the rest of the world. By the time the Bosnian Serbs declared their own independent state on January 9, 1992, the "Republika Srpska" had achieved exclusive Serbian television coverage over 70 percent of the former Bosnian Republic. The media space in Bosnia had been shattered by force before any territory was taken.

Throughout the conflicts that followed, media would become a weapon of war. In order to achieve a Greater Serbia, it was essential to extend the reach of Serbia proper, hence the strategy of ethnic cleansing. Serbian media saturated the airwaves with abominable propaganda in order to motivate Serb citizens to slaughter their Croat and Muslim neighbors, and to forcibly expropriate their homes and fields. Appealing to historic grievances and a mythology of victimization, Serbian state-run media created an atmosphere of fear and hatred among Yugoslavia's Orthodox Serbs by spreading "exaggerated and false messages of ethnically based attacks by Bosnian Muslims and Catholic Croats against Serb people," according to the indictment of Slobodan Milosevic for war crimes later handed down by the International Criminal Tribunal for the Former Yugoslavia.

Serb television reported that radioactive waste was

deliberately sowed over Serb farms, that a Croatian doctor was injecting pregnant women with a serum that would abort any male fetuses and, famously, that Bosnian Muslims were feeding Serb children to the lions in the Sarajevo Zoo. Serb journalists portrayed Bosnian Muslims as violent fundamentalist extremists and exaggerated the extent of Arabic-speaking volunteers from the Middle East and North Africa, called Mujahideen, who were fighting on their behalf. Radio Television Serbia (formerly Radio Television Belgrade) regularly broadcast footage of mutilated bodies and mass graves alleged to be the work of Muslims and Croats. Each side's propaganda fed the mass psychology of hatred.

Pulitzer Prize-winning journalist Roy Gutman, writing from Serb army headquarters in Banja Luka, described how a Serb propaganda officer began one such article: "Under a hot Balkanic sky necklaces have been strung of human eyes and ears, skulls have been halved, brains have been split, bowels have been torn out . . . and children's bodies have been pierced by bayonets."

One of the major turning points in the war was when Serb artillery slaughtered sixty-nine shoppers at the central Sarajevo marketplace, an atrocity that seemed to break through the psychological numbness of viewers worldwide. In response, commentators on Serb TV in Pale, the capital of Republika Srpska, blamed the attack on Muslim green berets who killed their own people to provoke a NATO intervention. Mladen Vuksanovic, an award-winning documentary film director, said of his former colleagues, "I am beginning to hate my profession from the bottom of my soul. They are not journalists, they are professional murderers."

International journalists, on the other hand, covered

the war with skill and courage. Their relentless reports from the besieged capital of Sarajevo often led the evening news, increasing the pressure on European and American diplomats who appeared incapable of action. Night after night, the world watched the wretched civilians of this once-beautiful city being cut down by snipers sitting safely in apartments on the hills above. Then, on August 2, 1992, a story by Roy Gutman in New York's *Newsday* shook the West's conscience; his exposé appeared under a banner headline with two-inch letters that read "THE DEATH CAMPS OF BOSNIA." Four days later, Penny Marshall of Independent Television Network (ITN), based in London produced video reports from one of these, the Omarska camp. The *Guardian* described the scene:

> *The men are at various stages of human decay and affliction; the bones of their elbows and wrists protrude like pieces of jagged stone from the pencil thin stalks to which their arms have been reduced...Their stares burn, they speak only with their terrified silence, and eyes inflamed with the articulation of stark, undiluted, desolate fear-without-hope.*

Video of the skeletal prisoners conjured up the searing images of the Holocaust as no print reporting could do. Jon Western, an American intelligence officer at the State Department who had been compiling evidence of the camps, wrote, "We had all the documentation we needed before. We knew all we needed to know. But the one thing we didn't have was videotape. We had never seen the men emaciated behind barbed wire. That was entirely new."

It would be three more years before NATO responded, however, seriously bombing Serb positions, which led to a negotiated end to the fighting. By failing to intervene, the international community was complicit in the violence that would leave hundreds of thousands dead and half the homes in Bosnia destroyed.

After years of ineffective diplomatic initiatives, a few weeks of aerial bombardment proved sufficient to bring the parties together in November 1995 in Dayton, Ohio to negotiate an end to the conflict. But with the war over, what could be done to break the cycle of violence and victimization that had bedeviled the Balkans for generations? And what would prevent the next round of grievances and retribution from escalating into yet another war?

War Crimes on Trial

Invoking the Convention on the Prevention and Punishment of the Crime of Genocide, passed by the UN General Assembly on December 9, 1948, the UN Security Council established the International Criminal Tribunal for the Former Yugoslavia (ICTY), the first war crimes tribunal since Nuremberg, set to begin on May 7, 1996. A month before the opening trial was about to start in the The Hague, it suddenly occurred to me that no one in Bosnia would be able to watch the trials. If there were ever to be any healing from the war, I believed, the victims would have to see that justice was served. Only media could do that. Similarly, it was imperative that citizens in Serbia, who had been led into war by historical grievances magnified by racist propaganda, have some access to an objective accounting of the war crimes committed in their names.

It seemed impossible to get the requisite permission, assemble a production crew, buy satellite time, arrange for local broadcasts, and raise money to cover the trial in just twenty-eight days. Fortunately, George Soros agreed within twenty-four hours to give $1 million to help make it happen.

The first person to be held accountable was Dusko Tadic. (He would be found guilty in May 1997. Two years later, Milosevic was indicted and died in prison in The Hague on March 11, 2006.) The UN was planning to record the trial with a sophisticated system of five cameras and permission was granted to rebroadcast their feed. Paul Mitchell, the director of the definitive television documentary series, *The Death of Yugoslavia,* oversaw the production. We also assembled a team of technicians from a dozen countries, brought in leading journalists and experts on the war, arranged rebroadcast rights from Bosnian state television and all five independent stations, and convinced the state broadcasting behemoth, NHK, in Hilversum outside The Hague, to use its technical facilities to receive the UN's signal and upload it to a satellite.

Despite a building the size of the Pentagon, NHK claimed not to have any spare space for us and we ended up setting up shop in one corner of their immense entry hall, which we walled off with black cloth. The most difficult challenge was getting the right satellite space, but we managed to solve it at the last minute with help from the EU's European Broadcast Service. There were countless issues to resolve, but when Dusko Tadic took the stand, we went live.

Every station in Bosnia retransmitted our signal for eleven hours a day, preempting other programming. Virtually every man, woman, and child in Bosnia were glued to their sets for the three-month trial.

"We always made sure there was one person left at home to watch the trials, if we had to go out," one Sarajevan explained.

"It was painful to watch the faces of these war criminals who had turned our world to hell, but the fact that they would be judged made me feel whole again. It was a kind of a cleansing of the soul." Television, which had played such a key role in promoting the war, would now be deployed to help bring about reconciliation and justice.

Where war crimes in the Balkans were inflamed by media, in Rwanda, hate media became the organizing tool for genocide.

Radio Genocide

For roughly five hundred years, Rwanda had been ruled by a hereditary Tutsi monarchy, although the Tutsis comprised only about 15 percent of the population. Hutu and Tutsi shared a common language, history and culture. They lived in the same communities, attended the same schools and churches, worked in the same offices, and often intermarried. Until 1959, there had been no systematic political violence between them. As anti-colonialist sentiment spread across Africa, however, demands for majority rule increased. In the so-called "Social Revolution" of 1959 to 1961, Belgian colonialists and Catholic missionaries helped replace the Tutsi chiefs with Hutus and established a democratic republic dominated by them. In the ensuing years, a pattern developed of attacks by exiled Tutsis, followed by reprisal massacres against local Tutsi communities. By 1986, a million Tutsis had fled, many into English-speaking Uganda.

On October 1, 1990, Tutsi refugees living in Uganda formed a rebel army, the Rwandan Patriotic Front (RPF), and invaded Rwanda. Only the direct intervention of French soldiers and advisors prevented the rebels from overrunning the country.

The attacks, and another large invasion in 1993 that nearly succeeded, forced hundreds of thousands of Hutus to flee their homes; by some accounts a million became internally displaced people. A ceasefire was arranged in July 1993, followed by a peace agreement brokered in Tanzania known as the "Arusha Accords," formally ending the war. These ensured the right of return for Tutsi refugees and established a blueprint for a broad-based transitional government. As part of the accords, the United Nations agreed to send a small peacekeeping force, the UN Assistance Mission in Rwanda (UNAMIR). Mindful of its recent dramatic failure to keep the peace in Somalia, the Security Council limited the force to a mere 2,548 troops.

Broadcasting Hatred

Four days after the signing, opponents of the accords established a new radio station in Kigali, Radio Television Libres des Mille Collines (RTML), and began broadcasting highly inflammatory messages against the Tutsis and the moderate politicians who supported a peace settlement. In time it became the most popular station in the country. RTML took its language and racist ideology from a newspaper called *Kangara* ("*Wake Up*") that started publishing after the February 1990 invasion by the RPF. Fearing defeat from this Tutsi army and the killings of Hutus that might follow, *Kangara* spewed ever more vicious propaganda against the Tutsis and began to suggest their elimination.

On October 21, 1993, shortly after the Arusha Accords had brought an end to the fighting in Rwanda, Tutsi army officers in neighboring Burundi (not associated with the Rwandan RPF) assassinated Melchior Ndadaye, the popular, newly elected Hutu president of this country, located just to the south of Rwanda, with a similar balance of Hutu and Tutsi. The assassination set off a series of massacres on both sides. Believing that the Tutsis could never be trusted, Hutu extremists began organizing a "Hutu Power" movement with support from Juvenal Habyarimana, the Rwandan president who had assumed power in 1973. Leaders of Hutu Power aligned with the governing party organized a militia of small neighborhood bands called the Interahamwe ("those who fight together"); these groups began compiling lists of Tutsis and moderate Hutus to be targeted and went on retreats to practice burning houses, throwing grenades, and hacking dummies with machetes.

In order to ensure the massacre of large numbers of Tutsis, RTML propagandists needed to demonize, delegitimize, and dehumanize them first. With a mixture of live music and chatty talk radio, announcers used colloquial speech to create a conversation with the Hutu population that was spiced with incendiary racist propaganda. Tutsis were described as collaborators of the RPF and called cockroaches, dogs, snakes, monkeys, cannibals, and hyenas. Announcers played on the memories of past domination before the Hutu majority came to power, incited fear of an RPF attack, invented massacres which had never taken place, and propounded theories of Tutsi foreignness that would justify their expulsion or extermination. Predictions of what might befall Tutsi communities and specific Hutu politicians were uncannily prescient, prompting Tutsis to carefully follow RTML in order to get a sense of upcoming actions.

Calls by Hutu Power extremists for the "total extermination" of the "inyenzi" (cockroaches) were repeated in public rallies and on the radio. For anyone interested in listening, there was no shortage of warnings of the approaching holocaust. Anti-Tutsi violence was increasing. Death squads were reported. Military officers were distributing weapons to civilians. The Interahamwe militia trained in the open.

On January 11, 1994, the commander of UNAMIR, Canadian Lieutenant General Romeo Dallaire sent an urgent fax to the Department of Peacekeeping Operations at UN headquarters in New York. He described in detail information he had received from a high level informant of death lists, arms caches, and plans to kill opposition leaders and Belgian soldiers in the hopes of provoking a civil war. But Kofi Annan, then the chief of UN peacekeeping forces, refused to act. In October 1993, videotapes of the killing of eighteen American Rangers serving alongside the UN force in Somalia, their bodies dragged through the streets of Mogadishu, were endlessly replayed on television sets around the world; and the UN, and especially the United States, had little appetite for any further interventions. The so-called "CNN effect," the theory that the twenty-four-hour news cycle constrained military and foreign policy makers, would show the perverse impact that media coverage could have.

Meanwhile, preparations for mass murder intensified. The Rwandan military began to arm local self-defense forces to supplement the party-run Interahamwe militia. But Colonel Theoneste Bagosora, one of the principal architects of the genocide, estimated he only had enough firearms for a third of his new recruits. Others would have to operate with traditional weapons: spears, bows and arrows, and machetes. Imports of machetes soared to more than five hundred thousand, one for every third Hutu male. Training for the militia and the new self-defense forces accelerated at the end of 1993 and beginning of 1994.

RTML's broadcast attacks on the Arusha Accords and incitement against the Tutsi population became ever more virulent. Announcers repeatedly claimed that the massacres of Hutus in Burundi were part of an imminent plot to exterminate Hutus from the entire region. On April 3, 1994, RTML announced that during the next three days "there will be a little something here in Kigali, and also on April 7 and 8 you will hear the sound of bullets or grenades exploding." On the very eve of the genocide, RTML talk show hosts viciously attacked the prime minister, Agathe Uwilingiyimana, claiming she was planning to assassinate the president and warned that his killing would be followed by the extermination of the entire Tutsi population. Rwanda's minister of information tried to reign in RTML, but the station had grown beyond the law, and he was one of the first people killed in the slaughter to follow.

Then on the evening of April 6, 1994 an airplane carrying Rwandan president Juvenal Habyarimana and Burundian president Cyprien Ntaryamira was shot down as it prepared to land in Kigali following their peace talks in Arusha, killing them both and igniting the genocide. Many suspected Colonel Bagosora was behind the assassinations.

One Hundred Days of Hell

Within an hour of the president's plane being shot down on April 6, the killings began. Roadblocks appeared throughout Kigali and a planned orgy of mass killings erupted throughout the country. This was not simply ethnic cleansing; this was a deliberate attempt to exterminate the minority Tutsi and moderate Hutu populations. The very first to be assassinated were Hutu opposition politicians, creating a political vacuum that Colonel Bagosora's allies used to seize power. At daybreak on April 7, ten Belgian soldiers guarding Prime Minister Uwilingiyimana were disarmed, taken to a military base, tortured, murdered, and mutilated, and Mrs. Uwilingiyimana, the prime minister, assassinated. The Belgians immediately withdrew their remaining troops, the core of the UN protection force, and the United States refused to authorize the deployment of reinforcements. The perpetrators of genocide would face no international interference.

The wholesale slaughter had been meticulously organized. Extermination lists had been prepared and army, national police, and militia members began killing thousands of Tutsis. But for the full scope of their plans to be realized, the perpetrators needed to mobilize large numbers of the civilian population. As the brilliant Polish journalist Ryszard Kapuscinski reflected,

> For the leaders of the regime had more than just the ultimate goal—the final solution in mind. On the road to the Highest Ideal, which was nothing less than the total annihilation of the enemy, it was critical that the nation be united in crime; through mass participation in the criminal act there would arise an all-unifying feeling of guilt, so that every citizen, having on his conscience another's death, would be haunted from that moment by someone else's inalienable right to retaliation, behind which he could glimpse the specter of his own end.

The task of mobilizing the masses of Hutus fell primarily to RTML and, to a somewhat lesser extent, to Radio Rwanda. "The graves are still only half full!" RTML pronounced. "Help us to fill them! Form barriers! Block the infiltration of the cockroaches!" RTML began broadcasting twenty-four hours a day. Throughout the one hundred days of hell, hate radio became what General Dallaire later called the "soundtrack of the genocide."

The iconic images of the genocide are of civilians at makeshift roadblocks brandishing machetes in one hand and portable radios in the other. "Whoever does not have his identity card should be arrested and maybe lose his head there," RTML advised. "Fight them with the weapons at your disposal; you have arrows, you have spears…Take up your traditional tools." Names were read of people identified as RPF "accomplices," marking them for extermination; listeners were encouraged to phone in with others. Announcers broadcast the exact hiding places of individuals, the locations where groups took shelter and even the license plate numbers of cars of people trying to flee. Requests from militia leaders for supplies or weapons were relayed over the air. Throughout the killing spree, RTML commentators congratulated the butchers for their heroism.

Failure to Respond

As reports of the massacre reached Washington, policymakers considered destroying RTML's antenna or jamming the hate radio broadcasts using Commando Solo, an Air National Guard EC-130E equipped for such a job. But despite urgent appeals from General Dallaire and deputy assistant secretary of state Prudence Bushnell, the National Security Council determined it was too expensive. "Within the third week of the genocide," reflected General Dallaire later, "when the UN had buckled under and decided that it was *not* going to reinforce the mission, that it was also going to abandon Rwanda, the only voice, the only weapon that I had, was the [international] media. If, through the media, I could shame the international community into acting, then I would have achieved my aim . . . . I felt that one good journalist on the ground was worth a battalion of troops." If Rwanda represents one of the most shameful episodes in international peacekeeping, or the lack thereof, it is also the poster child for the failure of the international news media. While the local media in Rwanda fueled the killings, the international media virtually ignored them. There were only two foreign journalists in Rwanda on April 6 when the genocide began. Throughout April there were never more than ten to fifteen reporters in the country at any time. The attention of the press was focused on the fighting in Bosnia, a "first world European conflict." Yet in a hundred days, four times as many civilians would be killed in Rwanda as died in the six years of fighting in Bosnia. The first satellite uplink did not arrive in Rwanda until late May, after the RPF had already secured the capital. The main story became the evacuation of foreigners. Unfortunately, most of the TV teams evacuated with them.

There are many explanations for the failure of the international press. Certainly, some of the blame is due to the long-term decline of foreign news coverage, a subject beyond the scope of this book. If fault were to be apportioned, it would lie more with out-of-country editors than the journalists on the ground. In a 2000 report for the International Press Institute, Alan Kuperman defined four journalistic lapses. "First it mistook genocide for civil war," persistently referring to "ancient tribal hostilities" instead of a methodical, planned extermination of a people. Second, was "to report that violence was on the wane when in fact it was mounting." The third reporting error was that "early published death counts were gross underestimates," and, finally, "Western news organizations focused almost exclusively on Kigali, a city that contained only 4 percent of Rwanda's population, and did not report the far broader tragedy unfolding around them." But perhaps the greatest cause for the media's failure in Rwanda, and subsequently the catastrophic lack of military intervention to stop the slaughter was the paucity of images. There were virtually no videos of the killings. This time, there would be no "CNN effect."

In mid-July, the genocide ended when the RPF defeated the Rwandan Army, provoking a massive exodus of nearly two million Rwandan Hutu refugees into neighboring countries. A cholera epidemic soon broke out in the refugee camps around Goma, causing thirty thousand deaths before it was brought under control. The international news media, having failed to adequately report the genocide, now found it convenient to cover the easierto-understand humanitarian crisis. Hordes of Western journalists swarmed into what was then called Zaire (now Congo); the story of the Hutu refugee tragedy completely overwhelmed any coverage of the genocide that produced it. With help from French forces occupying a third of Rwanda under the pretense of securing a humanitarian "safe zone" in *Operation Turquoise* toward the end of the genocide, most of the Rwandan genocide commanders were permitted to pass with their weapons into Zaire, sowing the seeds of wars that would continue to this day.

A Power to Heal

Paul Kagame, who led the victorious RPF army that ended the Rwandan holocaust and later became its president, was visiting the Yad Vashem Holocaust Memorial in 1995 to get ideas for a genocide museum in Rwanda when David Michaelis, then the producer of a popular Israeli television news program and a close friend and colleague of mine, stopped to talk with him. Michaelis told Kagame about Internews' broadcasts of the UN War Crimes Tribunal for the Former Yugoslavia from The Hague, which had only recently begun, and asked if he would support a similar effort for Rwanda. It was not an easy decision. In 1994, Rwanda was the only state to vote against the establishment of the Rwanda war crimes tribunal in the United Nations because the trials were to be based in Arusha, Tanzania, instead of Rwanda, and because the UN had refused to allow the death penalty. But Kagame liked the idea of broadcasting the proceedings and he wrote his name and a one-sentence note of support on a paper napkin that Michaelis handed him. Michaelis sent the napkin to me by DHL and the next day I flew from Paris, where I was living, to Kigali.

When I arrived at the Continental Hotel, there was a media circus going on. Fighting had broken out across the border in Kivu Province in Zaire and reporters were milling about. Satellite dishes had been installed on the lawn around the hotel. A British journalist offered the phone number for the minister of information. I went to my hotel room, dialed the minister's number and told the receptionist I was carrying a hand-written note from President Kagame. Five minutes later, when a limousine pulled up outside the hotel with the minister inside, I showed him the napkin; he smiled and told me we could expect the full support of his government.

When the UN's International Criminal Tribunal for Rwanda (ICTR) got started in 1997, Internews was the only organization prepared to videotape the proceedings. Whereas the ICTY in The Hague had five state-of-the-art robotic cameras, the Rwanda tribunal was provided only a single audio tape recorder. The institutional racism was blatant. Rwanda was intensely mistrustful of the United Nations, whose peacekeepers had pulled out during the genocide.

Kagame remained faithful to his word and allowed the video of the trials to be distributed without impediment. Television only reached a tiny percentage of people in the capital, so every other month Internews produced an edited compilation of the testimony in Arusha and showed it in villages throughout Rwanda on a large TV screen from the back of a pickup truck. People in the villages wore their Sunday best, giving the gatherings the feel of church. These videos were also aired in Rwanda's sixteen provincial prisons housing the 120,000 *genocideurs* awaiting trial for crimes against humanity. In the prisons, thousands of men, dressed in flamingopink uniforms, witnessed the trials of the leaders who had commanded them. After both the community and prison showings, we taped the audiences' questions and comments and played these for the judges and prosecutors back in Arusha, then returned to the villages and prisons with their answers. It offered a slow but effective dialogue between the court personnel and the nation on whose behalf they were working. Each month an average of twenty thousand people—both victims and perpetrators of the genocide—watched the documentaries.

When Wanda Hall, the project director, first started to produce and distribute these films, the goal was to educate the Rwandan population about the International Tribunal and how it functions with the national justice system. But she soon found something more profound was taking place. For a people who are information-starved and have no voice, the community and prison meetings provided a rare moment when their essential human dignity was affirmed. After a prisoner watched a video of Carla Del Ponte, the chief prosecutor of the war crimes tribunal, address a question he had asked at the previous meeting, the inmate exclaimed, "I am somebody. I exist."

A wizened old woman approached Hall at a village gathering to express her anger and frustration that former officials on trial in Rwanda were enjoying the comforts that international prison standards provided while the victims of their crimes continued to live in poverty. "Bagosora gets to take two hot showers a day. I have never had a hot shower in my life," she lamented. Part therapy session, part information sharing, the viewings created a unique feedback loop between the people who experienced the genocide and the prosecutors in Arusha. "It is somewhat presumptuous," commented Hall, "to think that we can bring about reconciliation with these videos, but providing a safe place for people to speak and be heard enriched their lives in ways we'll never fully understand."

The Way Forward

All the issues that had shocked the conscience of the world and led to the war crimes tribunal for Yugoslavia—racism, propaganda, mass murders and genocide—were more blatant, magnified, and deplorable in the case of Rwanda. The scale of the killing was far greater—up to eight hundred thousand slaughtered, as many as three-quarters of the minority Tutsi population—the sadistic hatred more palpable, and the failure of the international community to intervene to stop the genocide even more reprehensible and inexcusable.

The use of the media to incite hatred was similar in both countries; but in Rwanda it was more explicitly operational, directing listeners to commit specific acts of violence. Whereas the international media's coverage of Yugoslavia consistently and professionally exposed the atrocities, putting pressure on world leaders to act, in Rwanda, by contrast, the international media were largely absent and their reporting helped obfuscate, rather than clarify, what was taking place there.

The genocide in Rwanda offers the clearest example of how a governing force can use the media for evil. After Rwanda, hate media have been recognized by the International Criminal Court as possible prosecutorial acts of genocide. There have been some limited, but effective, uses of media monitoring to give early warnings of impending conflict or inter-communal violence. Much more could and should be done along these lines. There have been important policy debates about whether hate radio stations should be jammed, as was requested by the head of UN forces there and refused. Such an action will not by itself prevent atrocities or roll back military aggression, but it will help delegitimize and undermine the rationale that supports them. Exposure of atrocities by the international media can help bring outside pressure to bear on the perpetrators of war crimes as well.

Even more important, however, Rwanda is an extreme example of the danger of local media falling into the hands of a single sectarian faction. Conversely, a pluralistic media helps ensure that a marketplace of ideas will dilute any perversion of information. Where that is lacking, the abuse of the media is far more likely to occur. The single most effective way to stop civil wars and crimes against humanity is to establish a vibrant, independent and pluralistic media environment.

In both the former Yugoslavia and in Rwanda, media were instrumental in fomenting ethnic hatred and violence but also essential in the efforts at reconciliation that followed. If we are to understand the roots of conflict, more attention needs to be paid to media, and if we are to prevent conflict, more efforts to bolster media development must be made. Media also have a vital role to play in post-conflict reconstruction and the rebuilding of civil society. Much less understood is media's role in development. Conflict and underdevelopment go hand in hand. As we'll now see in Kenya, media have shown the potential to incite violent conflict, but are also at the forefront of dramatic changes now improving the lives of the poorest of the poor.

SILICON SAVANNAH

A revolution is brewing in the heart of Africa. Its aim is not the overthrow of corrupt governments or a redistribution of wealth, though its effects will undoubtedly bring political and economic reform in its wake. This new media Mecca is transforming Africa as profoundly as the end of colonialism did in the 1960s.

To travel to Kenya is to enter a state of cognitive dissonance. Known for its spectacular wildlife, its ethnic conflicts, and its massive corruption, Kenya is also home to a vibrant culture of digital development that has caught the tailwinds of modern media to leapfrog into the twenty-first century. Take a digital safari through Kenya's innovative start-ups and you'll see the first tender shoots of the new Africa. From crowd sourcing to mobile banking, Kenyans are world leaders in new technological applications for development. "We have so many problems," says Bitange Ndemo, the permanent state secretary in the Kenyan Ministry of Information and Communications, one of the improbable leaders of this revolution. "But this is precisely our greatest opportunity," he concludes with his characteristic optimism.

A large, avuncular man, Ndemo moves more like a prizefighter than a government minister. He is a man in a hurry with a determination that brooks no opposition. Born in Kisii, a city of eighty thousand in southwestern Kenya, Ndemo's father died when he was seven years old, leaving five wives and forty children.

Growing up, Ndemo had to wait for his older brother to finish high school before his family could afford to send him. He finally graduated, saved enough money to go to the US, and enrolled at the University of Minnesota. Eventually, he was awarded a Ph.D. in Industrial Economics from the University of Sheffield, England before settling into academic life as a professor of economics at the University of Nairobi.

Dr. Ndemo was inspired by the movie *Field of Dreams* and its prophesy, "If you build it, they will come." Ndemo's own dream was to catapult Kenyans out of their chronic underdevelopment by linking them to the worldwide revolution in digital communications technologies.

In 2005, he received an unexpected phone call from information minister Mutahi Kagwe congratulating him on his appointment as permanent secretary. In Kenya, the permanent secretary is responsible for the day-to-day operations of the Ministry. Such appointments are usually political. Selecting an academic like Ndemo signaled much was about to change in Kenya after the overthrow of its longtime strongman Daniel Arap Moi.

Laying the Foundation

In 2005, Kenya was a country in the midst of a democratic makeover. Two years earlier, Daniel Arap Moi, its corrupt and despotic president for twenty-five years, had ceded power to Mwai Kibaki. Moi had severely restricted Kenyans' access to information, clamping down on the country's few private television and radio broadcasters. "Under the Moi regime," said Davis Adieno, a former coordinator of the National Taxpayers Association, "the government was clearly on one side and the citizens on the other. Citizens had no business to access government information." But President Kibaki, also an economist by training, was a more practical man. He understood that fast-tracking Kenya for the new media and information revolution would benefit the economy. *Vision 2030*, the president's blueprint for transforming Kenya into a middle class country, published after the violence of the presidential elections of 2008, emphasized information and communications technology as vital to a knowledge-based economy.

When Ndemo joined the government, Kenya was near the bottom of African countries in terms of Internet connectivity. He was determined to vastly improve this by expanding the country's infrastructure and online content. With his audacious determination, Ndemo set out to connect Kenya to high speed fiber optic cables on the other side of the Indian Ocean and to launch sub-Saharan Africa's first Open Data Initiative to put all government information online through a free, public website (https://opendata.go.ke). He knew only an informed and connected citizenry could disrupt ageold patterns of poverty, poor education, and parochialism.

Increasing capacity would be the key to everything else, he believed, and bringing high-speed, fiber-optic cables to the country would be an essential first step. "We built the infrastructure when Kenya used only one gigabyte of capacity via the satellite," he recounted with a mischievous smile. "Critics did not see how we could put up three terabytes [3,000 times greater] when there was no demand. Even those who worked on the feasibility study thought I was crazy, but today the consumption trajectory is such that the private sector has found it worthwhile to invest in three other cables and last week another cable was started."

Ndemo did everything he could to sidestep the country's infamous bureaucracy. After attending meetings in five capitals over six months for a World Bank-funded regional cable initiative aimed at increasing bandwidth and capacity, he recognized the effort was not making any real progress and he impulsively pulled Kenya out of the project. "Realizing that the cost of the meetings had exceeded the cost of laying the fiber, I decided to give a quit notice," he told me. He endured a good deal of criticism, but finally convinced President Kibaki that Kenya should chart its own path and develop capacity on its own. "It is said that he who travels alone travels fastest," Ndemo likes to repeat. Without government funding, and having pulled out of the World Bank initiative, Ndemo nevertheless negotiated an agreement with the government of the United Arab Emirates, started work on the project with help from local service providers, and secured a loan from Citibank in the midst of the chaos and violence that engulfed Kenya after the election of 2007.

Almost overnight, information and communications technology became the fastest growing sector of Kenya's economy. The price of connectivity dropped by a factor of eighty. In 2005, it cost Kenya $4,000 per megabyte of broadband; now it is $50. As late as 2009, only one thousand Kenyans had broadband. Today the number is six million and climbing. The country has leaped ahead of South Africa with the highest percentage of Internet users on the continent.

But Ndemo, acutely attuned to the winds of technological change, realized the future was with mobile telephony, and he adroitly steered the country in its direction, bypassing not only landlines but computer accessed Internet as well. From 2009, when the first of four cables reached Mombasa on Kenya's east coast, to 2011, the number of mobile phone subscribers soared from seven million to thirty million. Voice and data over mobile phones now passed through fiber cables that hugely increased bandwidth, dramatically reducing the costs of making calls. It used to cost $6 per minute to call the US, but currently it is less than $.02. "There are now more mobile subscribers than adults in Kenya," noted Chelsea Clinton in an August 8, 2012 report for NBC News. The technology firms proliferating in Kenya's Silicon Savannah now design their products for mobile phones rather than computers. An astonishing 98.8 percent of Internet connections in Kenya are made over cell phones.

The revolution in new media is not only one of faster, slimmer gadgets. It is also a shift from a narrow, proprietary view of information to one that includes a free-flow of data. After exponentially increasing connectivity in Kenya, Ndemo turned his attention to creating a free and open portal for government data making it available to ordinary citizens. Information often translates into power, but in the new digital world one must embrace the notion that everyone benefits when access to information expands. It is a move from control to community. The democratization of information lays the foundation for digital citizenship. Access to government information can improve services and reduce the corruption that inhibits growth.

Soon after he was named permanent secretary, Ndemo went to see President Kibaki with the minister Ndemo served under,

Mutahi Kagwe. The president quickly agreed to Ndemo's plan to build a government open data portal. The United States had led the global open data movement, launching its data.gov site in 2009 (www.data. gov currently holds close to four hundred thousand data sets of US government information across all sectors), followed by the World Bank the next year. Thirty-one other countries created similar portals, but Kenya would become the first in Sub-Saharan Africa. With initial support from the top, Ndemo mapped out a strategy to neutralize the many obstacles he would inevitably confront. "In government, you seize the moment and the opportunity when you get it," Ndemo reflected. His method was simple. "You do the end first and then you can put the rest in place later."

Ndemo realized that once something has been measured, it could be changed. Correlations of data can reveal causal connections that can identify where to apply the appropriate remedies. One of the problems with Kenya's government data is it existed in "silos," each ministry jealously guarding its own information. This only increased opportunities for mismanagement, the misappropriation of funds, and bribery. Putting government information in a single, searchable portal would allow applications to be developed that could explore trends gleaned from census reports, economic, health, and education data. But opening government data to the public in one easily accessible portal would also reveal failures and favoritism that could make enemies.

An early battle came with the Ministry of Lands, which was reluctant to digitize its data because, historically, land grabbing and corruption in land allocation has been a major source of revenue for top officials and middle-range civil servants. But when Ndemo's ministry began to automate land transactions and make them easily searchable by digitizing them, property tax revenues jumped from eight hundred million Kenyan shillings to over eight billion. Several of his staff quit after they received death threats from angry citizens. When Ndemo began mapping poverty and showed where members of Parliament were distributing the 2.5 percent of the country's tax revenues they controlled through the Constituencies Development Fund, a discretionary fund that was supposed to be directed at poverty reduction programs, the MPs came down on him. Still, he persisted.

Ndemo has no patience for government bureaucracies, which are notoriously slow. One of his favorite sayings is "A rolling stone gathers no moss." "If I move fast enough," he once confided in me, "I can present my opponents with a fait accompli." Rather than base the Open Data Initiative on Kenya's Freedom of Information Act, which had been languishing for years in the parliament, he tied it to the new 2010 constitution, which guaranteed every citizen the right to access information held by the State. In order to launch the site with the least amount of resistance, Ndemo decided to initially only use data already in the public domain and accept data in any format, from electronic to paper copies. Knowing young software designers would make the site more popular and user-friendly, Ndemo focused on data he thought critical for application development: the census, audited public financial accounts, performance results at schools and health facilities, and surveys of household income and spending.

Still, he ran into resistance from ministries fearing release of their data. He spent hours sitting in various ministry offices refusing to leave until he got his way. One of the ministries with the greatest share of government data was also the most recalcitrant. After several sit-ins, Ndemo finally got the chance to demonstrate for the minister on his own iPad how the site might utilize the information already in the public domain and secured his approval. But Ndemo's greatest tactic was to get an early commitment from the president to attend the Open Data Initiative launch and he used that to force the support of any remaining holdouts in the cabinet. "I announced the launch date [when the president would attend]," he said. "Things work better under crisis in government, and that is what helped me. You have to create a super crisis and say, 'The president is going to launch, and I don't know why you are refusing to give data.' Eventually they caved in."

With President Kibaki on board, and after the Planning Ministry released the 2009 census, Ndemo formed a task force to prepare the Website. He bypassed civil servants and pulled in a team of twenty-three volunteers who had collaborated with him in the past—data experts, software programmers, public officials and colleagues from Google and the World Bank. They pulled together two hundred data sets organized into six categories: education, health, energy, population, poverty, and water and sanitation.

The day before the launch, however, President Kibaki summoned Ndemo to his office to tell him the portal had been cancelled. In the room with the president were most of his senior ministers. They told Ndemo they were afraid the Open Data Initiative would undermine national security and expose the government to criticism. Ndemo argued that all the information was already in the public domain: anyone could see it, if they wished to. The meeting was supposed to last just twenty minutes, but Ndemo and his team pressed on. Employing various Google applications, they demonstrated how data sets could be used to predict service delivery gaps or how open data could help better allocate resources. "Look at the ratio of students versus teachers, energy resources based on census results. Look at boy-to-girl ratios regionally, by county, and you can see interesting correlations and areas that should be prioritized," one of his team leaders explained. The team presented maps that overlaid capital expenditures and population, clearly showing where shortfalls lay. The president and virtually all of the officials present were economists. Rather than make the case for greater transparency of government, Ndemo emphasized the economic benefits of open data and how it would increase employment. "The portal will change the lives of Kenyans," Ndemo argued passionately.

After more than two hours, the president relented and said he would attend the launch as scheduled. The next day, three thousand people gathered for the event. "Until the time I saw his vehicle, I was thinking someone is going to tell him not to come. But he actually came and launched the portal and completely changed a lot of things," Ndemo said with mischievous delight.

The new portal immediately showed its potential. By overlaying graphic visualization of data sets, patterns emerged and policy makers could more clearly see where best to focus the country's resources. As predicted, software developers immediately began writing code for dozens of new applications. At the iHub, an open innovation space for technologists, investors, tech companies, and hackers in Nairobi, the Open Data Initiative was like candy for a kid. Agriculture, which employs three-quarters of Kenya's population, would especially benefit from the new information solutions. "Using data collected from the agricultural sector and independent research institutions regarding the different types of soils in Kenya," noted Ndemo, "one group had been able to create an application that uses GPS to track a farmer's location, then offer the best solution or advice regarding what crops would do well in that area, or what type of fertilizer is best for the soil to increase productivity."

Another app called Huduma (Swahili for "service") enables people to report on the performance of public services in their district by text, e-mail, or Twitter to improve them, especially in the areas of education, governance, health, infrastructure, or water. The messages are routed to the appropriate authorities for action and their response time is published online. A citizen can send an SMS text message to the number 3018 to report a problem—potholes, leaky classrooms, demands for bribes, etc.—and the reports are aggregated and mapped on the Huduma site using Ushahidi's crowd sourcing software for public viewing. Erik Hersman, co-founder of Ushahidi (Swahili for "testimony" or "witness"), a Website for building open-source mapping, said, "There will be a dashboard which will compare one district with another. We will also layer in other information such as aid flows from, say, the World Bank. So, for example, if you pull up the profile of a school or clinic, you will have information about what aid it may have received as well as local reports on whether the teachers are turning up to work."

Kenya's Open Data Initiative is an immense political achievement. It gives government policymakers far greater clarity about the state of Kenya's economy and social development and provides citizens with unparalleled transparency that can improve government accountability. In addition, it will help to battle one of Kenya's greatest stumbling blocks to economic growth: corruption. Publishing open bids and government procurement records online will eliminate enduring opportunities for large-scale corruption, but such moves also threaten entrenched interests in Kenyan politics. Already, Ndemo has secured the president's written directive to put the personal financial records of all ministers and high government employees online. If these initiatives are fully implemented, Kenya's democratic future will be more secure and its economic health is likely to grow significantly. When asked by Chelsea Clinton what challenges technology and open data do not solve, Ndemo replied, "Good governance." Indeed, the economic potential of the Silicon Savannah could disappear if Kenya fails to reform a system of political patronage that exacerbates ethnic conflict.

Kenya's Darkest Hour

Ndemo's optimism is infectious. Following him around, it is easy to forget just how challenging Kenya's problems really are. The promise is there and the potential is truly revolutionary. But corruption, poverty and, perhaps most important of all, historical tribal conflicts present persistent obstacles. Following the disputed presidential election in December 2007, Kenya experienced the worst political violence in its recent history. Supporters of President Kibaki's opponent, Raila Odinga, claimed the ruling party stole the election through massive fraud (though subsequent analysis showed fraud on both sides made the actual results impossible to determine). Declared the winner on December 30 by the government's Electoral Commission, Kibaki immediately took the oath of office, setting off wide-scale rioting. The first attacks were against the president's supporters in neighborhoods that were predominantly Kikuyu, the largest ethnic group in Kenya (22 percent). Revenge attacks against Luo and Kalenjin communities, the next largest ethnic groups, rapidly transformed the fighting into outright intercommunal conflict.

Live television coverage showed horrifying scenes of police brutality, fires, and mayhem. Afraid live TV reports were inciting violence, the late Hon. John Michuki, the minister for internal security and Ndemo's direct superior at the time, banned any further television broadcasts of demonstrations and riots. Radio became the main source of information, with very mixed results.

A 2004 media law had led to a space of privately owned, local language radio stations targeting listeners from each of the main ethnic groups. Many of these vernacular radio station announcers had openly sided with one candidate or another and now incited their communities with language reminiscent of the hate messages that fueled the genocide in Rwanda. In particular, Kass FM, the most popular Kalenjin radio station in the heart of the Rift Valley, where some of the worst atrocities took place, was widely blamed for having contributed to a climate of fear and hate with its derogatory language against Kikuyus. Presenters routinely called for their expulsion, increasing tensions that eventually exploded in violence. Other stations, like the Kikuyu-language Kameme FM and Inooro FM, the Kalenjin station Chamge FM, and the Luo station Ramogi FM, were also accused of airing inflammatory broadcasts. There were many exceptions: several community and local language stations did much to promote reconciliation and defuse tension, particularly after the initial wave of violence in January 2008.

The most egregious hate speech took place during talk shows and call-in programs. "Suddenly, and largely accidentally, these talk shows had become an outlet for a public debate and an expression of voice which had been suppressed for decades," noted a BBC report on the violence. "Many of these voices were angry, disaffected and determined for change. Such outlets were arguably much needed, if tensions were to be defused through public debate rather than violence. In any society, such debate in an emotionally charged political environment would have required skillful and careful moderation." But few radio hosts had any training in conflict reporting or knew how to facilitate public debate. Indeed, not many were journalists; most were entertainers or disc jockeys with little understanding of the ethos of journalistic objectivity.

Several media experts who testified after the violence have argued the problem with vernacular radio stations was that they were privately owned and had a built-in incentive to promote sensationalism in their quest for a larger audience share. On the other hand, non-profit community stations, although tiny compared to their commercial sisters, played an exemplary role in trying to calm tensions and encourage reconciliation. A much-cited example is Pamoja FM, located in the Kibera slum on the edge of the capital, Nairobi, where some of the first conflicts broke out. Tole Nyatta, then a popular radio personality, ran a call-in show from 6 to 10 p.m. each evening, passionately exhorting his listeners not to react violently. Accosted on the street and subject to repeated death threats, Nyatta helped bring a measure of calm to a community that had suffered riots, police brutality, and constant provocations. "More community media could have quelled the violence," he argued.

The fighting threatened to unravel Kenya's precarious multicultural society. In January 2008, as news of the inflammatory role of many vernacular radio stations reached the government, authorities banned any further live radio broadcasts for a month. Apparently this backfired, as the media blackout only magnified people's fears. With radio and television both curtailed, citizens turned to their cell phones for information and this contributed to a rash of rumors that did nothing to ease tensions.

Objective information was difficult to find during the violence, making it harder for policymakers and the general public to know how to navigate through the crisis. Ory Okolloh, a human rights activist, lawyer, and blogger, suggested using a Website to aggregate eyewitness citizen reports of violent incidents from emails or SMS text messages on an interactive map in near-real time. In her blog post from January 3, 2008, four days after the outbreak of violence, she appealed for help: "It occurs to me that it will be useful to keep to a record [of the violence], if one is thinking long-term. For the reconciliation process to occur at the local level, the truth of what happened will first have to come out. Guys looking to do something— any techies out there willing to do a mashup of where the violence and destruction is occurring using Google Maps?" Two programmers, Erik Hersman and David Kobia, set to work writing code and in two sleepdeprived days built Ushahidi.com.

Ushahidi was not the first open-source map, but it launched a new field of crisis mapping for emergency responders. Its information proved faster and more reliable than the mainstream media in reporting acts of violence and pinpointing their locations, according to a later study by Harvard's Kennedy School of Government. Even though at the time few people in Kenya had access to it, the Ushahidi maps helped provide a more objective picture of what was actually happening. "We believe the number of deaths being reported by the government, police, and media is grossly under reported," blogged Okolloh after Ushahidi went online. "We also don't think we have a true picture of what is really going on—reports all of us have heard from family and friends in affected areas suggest things are much worse than what we have heard in the media."

By the time UN Secretary General Kofi Annan helped negotiate a power-sharing agreement on February 28, 2008, more than twelve hundred Kenyans were dead and five hundred thousand were left homeless. Fallout from the 2007-2008 violence continues to roil Kenyan politics to the present day. Four years after the disputed election, the International Criminal Court (ICC) in The Hague indicted four prominent Kenyans on charges of crimes against humanity for their roles in the post-election violence. Two of them, Uhuru Kenyatta and William Ruto, were sent to The Hague for the pretrial hearings in the midst of their campaign for the presidency in 2013 (both were later elected). Another charged by the ICC was the radio presenter of Kass FM, Joshua Arap Sang, who was accused of "coordinating the attacks using coded messages through his morning program." Sang's indictment highlighted the role of the media in the violence.

The mass media can play a vital role in peace-building only when it is seen as an objective arbiter of reliable information. But journalists, like anyone in a local crisis, are themselves influenced by the events swirling around them. Even in mainstream newsrooms across Kenya, the ethnic conflict strained relationships. Many journalists began to converse with their associates in their native dialect, raising tensions with fellow staff used to speaking with colleagues in Swahili or English, the common tongues. On air, subtle phrases and even body language can be provocative. Few Kenyan radio presenters and TV journalists possessed the skills to report on ethnic violence in ways that would not further inflame the conflict, nor did they have any training in conflict-sensitive journalism.

But if media, and in particular the vernacular media, could be a vehicle for escalating ethnic conflict, conceivably it could also be used to encourage greater tolerance. While tensions were still high, on January 30, 2008, Internews hosted a meeting of national and community media representatives, bloggers, and political commentators. Seventy-five media professionals came together for several days in a sometimes-painful self-appraisal of their own responsibilities, agreeing to participate in a comprehensive training program on conflict-sensitive journalism.

This particular methodology is based on a model developed by three South Africans to help journalists bring together communities after Apartheid. It had proved useful following the Rwandan genocide and during the 2002 war of independence in East Timor and would become an important tool in the post-election reconciliation process in Kenya. The methodology teaches journalists skills to analyze and understand conflict dynamics in their communities and to use language that does not stigmatize but allows for careful exploration of root causes. It emphasizes the mediator role journalists can play within communities in conflict. Participants were determined not to repeat their mistakes the next time Kenyans go to the polls.

Two other NGOs, Search for Common Ground and Media Focus on Africa, sought to address the roots of the conflict, developing and producing a series of television and radio soap operas focusing on the underlying issues in Kenyan society contributing to inter-ethnic tensions. Centered on a fictional football team, the Imani (Faith) Football Club, *The Team* dramatized real life interactions between players and coaches from different ethnic backgrounds. Produced and acted by Kenyans, *The Team* aired on Citizen TV, a popular station, and on Radio Jambo. Its ratings consistently placed it among the top ten programs in the country. Combining the world's most popular sport, football, with one of the world's most popular entertainment forms, the soap opera, *The Team* has spawned versions in seventeen countries. Each episode reinforces a common theme about the need for tolerance; if team members do not cooperate, they will not score goals.

From cell phones to soap operas, Kenya's destiny is being shaped by media. Poised between its tribal past and its aspirations for modernity, Kenya is on the cusp of a tectonic shift. The parochialism, corruption and patronage that have inhibited Kenya's development will not disappear overnight. Cultural memes are resistant to change, but change is coming. Information and communications technology can be part of the solution, but only if there are leaders like Bitange Ndemo who can dream big enough and get things done. His latest vision is Konza Techno City, Kenya's version of Silicon Valley, a $7 billion, five-thousand-acre technology hub forty miles south of Nairobi. It will provide two hundred thousand jobs. Already, several multinational corporations have announced plans to base their African headquarters there, and with commercial office space in short supply in the capital, more ICT firms are expected to set up shop. It is a grandiose vision, but knowing Ndemo, he will build it and they will come.

AFTER THE DELUGE

Previous chapters have focused on the role media have played in supporting movements for democracy, in building civil society, in fomenting and preventing conflict, and in promoting post-conflict justice and reconciliation. As mentioned, media also have the potential to transform development. Perhaps no other situation demonstrates more clearly the need for policymakers to take media into account than our traditional approach to humanitarian emergencies.

Depending on the crisis and the international media attention, most international humanitarian aid organizations – such as Oxfam and Save the Children— are relatively well-funded, sophisticated operations possessing logistics skills, the envy of many an army. Well-honed information systems allow them to collect and analyze critical data quickly and communicate effectively among staff members and with their home offices and the Western news media. They do important, life-saving work. Surprisingly, though, many of these groups mostly ignored the local media, which could provide the most effective outreach and dissemination of life-saving information as well as act as a source of unparalleled intelligence. The reasons why humanitarian aid organizations have not, until very recently, turned to local media, however, are understandable when one considers the changes that were transforming the media since the early 1990s after the collapse of the Soviet Union. In Indonesia, for example, like most of the developing world, local independent media were still an entirely new phenomenon. Indigenous, independent radio and television stations began emerging there only after the overthrow of General Suharto in 1998.

The basic media paradigm at the turn of the century was still a "one-to-many" model—very few national networks broadcasting to a mass, passive audience. This centralized approach drove every aspect of media for development, from diplomacy and public health campaigns to humanitarian relief. After the sudden expansion of local media that followed the fall of the Soviet Union, however, experts in foreign assistance began to consider the potential of using local media for development. The first tentative steps to remedy this in the humanitarian assistance sector came in response to one of the worst natural disasters of modern times—the 2004 tsunami in the Indian Ocean that slammed into Aceh, Indonesia on the northern end of Sumatra with the force of a thousand atomic bombs, killing 230,000 people.

Forty-five hundred miles away in New South Wales, Australia, Kathleen Reen was preparing her family's Christmas Day feast when she heard the news about the tsunami on the radio. Home for the holidays from her Internews base in Jakarta, Reen had been supporting the development of independent media in Indonesia since the overthrow of President Suharto and she had many friends and colleagues in the civil war-torn state of Aceh. She had trained journalists there in crisis reporting, but the news of the tsunami foretold a humanitarian disaster of unprecedented size and complexity. Twenty-four hours later, she was on a plane to Jakarta to gather the equipment and gear she would need to help with the relief effort.

As she flew into Banda Aceh, the district capital, the extent of the destruction was horribly evident from the air. Huge chunks of the coastline had been chewed away, parts of roads now headed directly into the sea only to pop out a few hundred yards later. Nearly 80 percent of the city had been destroyed. A conservative Sunni Muslim community, the Acehnese had fought an on-and-off again insurgency for greater autonomy during the previous thirty years, but the tsunami ended the conflict. Many of the most important leaders on both sides of the war disappeared that day. So did most of the journalists.

The first night Reen was in Banda Aceh, she stopped at an outdoor kiosk where there was a small television set connected to a satellite dish and a car battery. As she watched the evening news, she realized, "The national media in Jakarta are reporting this like it's in another country. They're not giving any information that is useful to the people here." The Acehnese needed timely, accurate, and welltargeted information as much as they needed food, water, and shelter; but without a functioning local media, they might as well have been watching foreign news reports. Reen's job was to try to get the local media back on its feet as quickly as possible so it could impart the vital information people needed, from where to get safe drinking water to how to find missing loved ones to what aftershocks might still be to come.

The challenge was monumental. Most infrastructure was destroyed. The journalists who did survive, who normally would be reporting the news, were themselves part of the disaster-affected population. A half-million people were left homeless. Everyone had lost family members. Jobs no longer existed. Water and food were in very short supply. Survivors spoke more of the dead than the living. Thousands wandered like zombies in a state of shock. Familiar landmarks were gone. Aceh had become a living ghost town.

Reen arrived in Aceh with enough food and water for a week and settled in a house about three kilometers from the coast. She hired a car and a driver, a young man in his early thirties whose mother and two sisters were missing. In one of the first radio stations she visited, Reen discovered the senior manager sitting alone on the second floor of the building, devastated. He had lost most of his staff and saw his life's work destroyed. He took her downstairs where dozens of people had been trapped the morning of the tsunami—they remained mummified, stuck in a macabre upsidedown deluge of furniture and mud.

Later, Reen went looking for the survivors of Prima FM, one of the stations with whom she had worked most closely before the tsunami. It was destroyed, and the four staff members who had been at work early that morning were killed. She eventually found the home of the station owner and sat with him while he cried, finally convincing him that he needed to get his station back on the air as soon as possible. "Let's do it here," he said, and they built it right on the spot. Reen had brought with her a portable "radio in a suitcase" that would make do until a stronger, more powerful transmitter could be located. When that arrived, Prima FM took the suitcase radio to the Indonesian government's nightly briefings and relayed live coverage back to the station.

But the need for information far outstripped the resources

of one station; Reen helped organize a large emergency radio station inside an abandoned education department building that had its own broadcast facilities. Groups of local journalists came and set up a newsroom in a cavernous meeting hall. The Radio Station Association of Indonesia got involved and sent volunteers from all over the country to help. Operating twenty-four hours a day, the station provided essential information to the survivors of the tsunami and became an unofficial communications center for the UN-coordinated relief efforts. (Official UN "recognition" of the need to communicate with disaster-affected populations through local media would not be given until the earthquake in Haiti five years later.)

Reen would check in at UN headquarters daily. Once, she noticed a large cardboard box filled with Ericsson mobile phones, ubiquitous in Jakarta. An Ericsson rep had made the donation and Nigel Snoad, a computer science engineer leading the UN Joint Logistics Centre, gave them to Reen who volunteered to buy SIM cards and distribute the phones to every journalist reporting on the emergency since few had working phones after the disaster. Satellite phones used by humanitarian NGOs were great for communicating internationally, but they were too expensive to be of much use in the local environment.

Indonesians were a texting-obsessive country well before the US and the cost of the technology was minimal. Reen brought in Chris Walker, a young American programmer, from Paris, who quickly designed an SMS news aggregator to allow the creation of a virtual mini-news information service where messages could be exchanged among many journalists at a time. "It was an *Aha!* moment," exclaimed Reen. The cell phone-based text messaging network allowed journalists to share information gathered from disparate sources—village chiefs, heads of NGOs, government and police officials, or the local imam—with their colleagues, greatly improving the quality of information survivors received. In addition, it acted as an informal feedback mechanism, giving recipients of humanitarian assistance a means to communicate their concerns through participating journalists to the UN and NGOs, which also had access to the SMS network. It proved relatively easy, for example, for people to alert rescue crews of gas leaks and unsafe structures or where food supplies had run out.

It may seem obvious that the people who most needed information were the survivors themselves and giving them a voice in the delivery of aid could be invaluable, but little had been done before to achieve this.

From Aceh to Haiti

Aceh suffered the worst damage from the tsunami; but a thousand miles away, giant waves triggered by the 9.0 earthquake also crashed against the coast of Sri Lanka, killing thirty-five thousand people and displacing another half-million.

Jacobo Quintanilla was a twenty-four-year-old journalist working in Spain for the media unit of the NGO ActionAid when the tsunami swept across the Indian Ocean. He flew to Sri Lanka and quickly became ActionAid's communications team leader. Quintanilla had grown up wanting to be a foreign correspondent, but his experiences in Afghanistan, Pakistan, Thailand, and the Maldives convinced him that local journalists in crisis situations were able to have a more direct impact on people's lives. "In emergencies," he reflected, "people are living in a black hole of fear and despair and they need information from local media to assess the dangers they continue to face, to locate family members and to know where to turn for help. In an emergency, information is king."

Quintanilla stayed in Sri Lanka for five years after the tsunami, running a humanitarian information and news service for internally displaced people, until he got a call from a colleague, Alison Campbell. "There's just been a devastating earthquake in Haiti," she said, and asked him to join an emergency media team leaving for the island immediately. It was Tuesday, January 12, 2010. He packed some clothes, a tiny laptop, ten-feature phones, and a first-aid kit in a small backpack and flew as soon as he managed to get a one way ticket from Colombo to Santo Domingo, capital of the Dominican Republic. There he met for the first time Mark Frohardt, the team leader for the Haiti response, whom Quintanilla knew only as a legend in the humanitarian relief community.

Frohardt had a reputation as a tough, innovative field operator and strategist. He had worked closely with Fred Cuny, the renowned disaster relief specialist who had revolutionized many of the fundamental concepts of humanitarian assistance. Cuny attracted worldwide fame when he miraculously managed to construct an underground water system that relieved the besieged city of Sarajevo during the war in Yugoslavia and then disappeared on a mysterious and ultimately fatal mission to bring an end to the fighting in Chechnya. Frohardt went on to Rwanda to help run the United Nations Human Rights Field Operations after the genocide of 1995.

Cuny taught Frohardt the importance of involving people in crisis in the design and implementation of humanitarian assistance, a lesson that Frohardt applied to media and information systems. "The people most affected by a disaster are also the ones who have the best information," he told me. "They know the culture, the language, the land and, most importantly, they know what they need. That is why it is so vital to empower local media, particularly radio, in a crisis. Interactive digital technologies are now vastly increasing the potential to engage them."

As soon as Quintanilla met him in Santo Domingo, they bought food and water, sleeping bags, a generator, computers, tape recorders, and lots and lots of energy bars. "I pretty much survived on those bars for the next six weeks," recalled Quintanilla.

Because Frohardt and Quintanilla could draw from a standby emergency response fund set up for Internews by the MacArthur Foundation, they were able to move quickly after the earthquake. Humanitarian relief organizations routinely operate with revolving accounts, allowing them to act first and raise additional reserves later, but this was the first fund of its kind to support a media intervention and it saved precious time that would have been spent fundraising.

In a stroke of good timing, just days before the earthquake at a meeting in London, some of the major relief and media development organizations had launched the Communicating with Disaster Affected Communities (CDAC) network to improve the communication flow between relief organizations and affected populations, an initiative funded by the Lodestar Foundation. When the disaster struck Haiti, the UN asked CDAC to serve as its communications cluster, where aid agencies came together to share information, a recognition of the vital role local media can play in providing life-saving information, and as a sounding board for the surviving population. CDAC would provide a vital coordination function for the various media support organizations working in Haiti.

The 7.2 magnitude earthquake that struck Haiti was the worst humanitarian crisis since the Indian Ocean tsunami, with a similar number of people killed, about 230,000. But unlike Aceh, where few bodies were recovered—most had been dragged out to sea, taking a devastating emotional toll on the survivors—in Haiti dead bodies were ever present.

Frohardt and Quintanilla headed to the airport where the military, relief organizations, and the media were setting up shop. The capital itself would have had trouble supporting this massive influx. Crucial buildings and infrastructure had been badly damaged or destroyed, including the UN headquarters, the National Palace, the parliament and twenty-eight of twenty-nine government ministries. An estimated eighteen thousand civil servants had also been killed.

The scene at the airport was chaotic; helicopters and planes were constantly landing and taking off. Tents were hurriedly being assembled under Klieg lights, satellite dishes were being hoisted into place, and people were rushing about with frantic energy.

The two quickly found Philippe Allouard at the airport. Allouard, who survived the earthquake, would die in a traffic accident in Haiti three years later on March 9, 2013. A Frenchman who had been living and working in Haiti for the previous twelve years, Allouard had been Internews' country director since 2009, a passionate journalist and enthusiastic advocate for humanitarian communications work in the country. He had been riding home on the back of a moto-taxi when the quake struck. Running over to assist a dying young man, he barely managed to escape on the motorbike as a flash flood roared down the street, killing everyone in its wake. The next day Allouard was already at work with Quintanilla, setting up an emergency radio program.

Operating from a makeshift media center set up by the media NGO Reporteurs Sans Frontiers in the first days after the earthquake, Frohardt's team did a quick assessment of the state of the various radio stations. With Allouard's years in Haiti and Quintanilla's deep experience in humanitarian information programming and a team of Haitian journalists, they produced *Enfomasyon Nou Dwe Konnen*, Creole for *News You Can Use*, a daily program providing critical information about water distribution points, displaced persons, and public health advisories. There had been close to three hundred radio stations in Haiti when the disaster hit, twenty-one of them in Port-au-Prince, but only one, Signal FM, never went off the air during the quake. Nine days later when other stations went back up on the air, eleven of them were able to broadcast the program, delivered on CDs by motorbike couriers. Weeks later, forty-one stations aired it, as did Radio France Internationale. *News You Can Use* became one of the most recognized programs in Haiti and a much-needed source of trusted information.

While a great deal of media attention in the West focused on the astonishing array of innovative uses of digital technologies in the crisis, radio was by far the most effective means of delivering information. "Radio stations are holding the country together," Carla Bluntschli, an American expat living in Haiti for twenty-five years, told the Associated Press. "They're kind of replacing the government, in a sense." The most effective radio station in the crisis was undoubtedly Signal FM. "Day and night, journalists and disc jockeys announce names of missing persons and news of open stores and dead celebrities, while calmly taking frantic calls and emails from both home and abroad," reported the AP. "Outside, people crowd the station's parking lot with crumbled hand-written notes, pleading for the announcers to read the names of their missing loved ones or a location where hungry people need relief." "Without the radio station, the country is dead," said the head of a church aid program. "Without the radio station, we can't communicate. We don't have anything."

A Digital Laboratory

But while radio proved to be the most effective tool for reaching the affected population, Haiti became a living laboratory for the use of new digital applications and mobile telephony that hold great promise for the future of emergency assistance. As we learned when the World Trade Center was attacked in New York on September 11, 2001, emergency communications systems proved wholly inadequate. Police and firefighters used different radio frequencies, making it difficult to communicate with each other. First responders, the military, and relief workers had no way of coordinating their efforts. People searching for missing loved ones were reduced to taping flyers to store windows. The one platform that proved remarkably useful was mobile phones.

Given that 85 percent of Haitians had access to mobile phones at the time of the earthquake, cell phones were an obvious tool. The ubiquity and interactivity of cell phones offered unprecedented opportunities for the delivery of disaster relief. The Comcel-owned mobile carrier Voilà restored service within twenty-four hours of the quake, and Digicel was back online a few days later. Here was a platform that could establish a dialogue between the disaster-affected population and the providers of humanitarian aid, instead of the one-to-many model that had characterized relief operations up to that point.

After the earthquake struck Haiti, so close to the United States and its large Haitian population, an unprecedented outpouring of volunteers participated in the relief efforts by writing software, establishing SMS information services, raising funds online, translating text messages, or designing crowd-sourced maps to aid relief crews. When news of the disaster reached Patrick Meier, then a graduate student at the Fletcher School of Diplomacy at Tufts University in Boston, he swung into action. Part of the team that developed the crowd mapping site Ushahidi, designed to map the violence erupting after the 2007 election in Kenya, Meier knew exactly how useful crisis mapping could be in a humanitarian emergency. Graphic overlays of information could show in a glance where aid was most needed. He called David Kobia, Ushahidi's lead tech developer, and within an hour, they posted a Ushahidi Website for Haiti. Ushahidi's Brian Herbert quickly wrote the software for an online microtasking tool that geo-tagged data about the needs for rescue, food, water, and security and graphically represented it on an online map.

Clusters of incidents identified by their location would point rescue teams to the most acute problem areas and individual calls for help could, theoretically, be acted upon by humanitarian organizations. An overlay of reports of water shortages, for example, could let relief organizations see where such problems were the worst. Many of the initial reports involved urgent pleas to be rescued. One of the first text messages, for example, read "To anyone in the Mont Joli-Turgeau area. . . . Jean-Olivier

Neptune is caught under rubbles of his fallen house . . . he is, but in very bad shape, please, please, please hurry."

For a crowd-sourced map that could aggregate input from many sources to work, though, there would have to be a massive system to translate thousands of messages from Creole to English, tag reports with geo-markers and provide a simple, well-publicized number for sending and receiving text messages. Meier sent a request for help to the Fletcher School Listserv. More than three hundred Tufts students volunteered to enter data. Rob Munro, a graduate student in computational linguistics at Stanford University, recruited one thousand Haitian Creole speakers in the US, Canada, and Europe to help with translation from the Creole. Katie Stanton, a US State Department officer, and Josh Nesbit at Frontline SMS, a free open-source software company, convinced the Haitian telecom Digicel to make the number 4636, called an SMS short code, available to the public for free. The number was massively promoted through local media. Initially, Ushahidi depended on phone calls and press reports, but once the SMS short code was activated, incident reports began to flow in greater numbers. A Haitian community organization called Block by Block picked up the Ushahidi template and was able to turn its detailed neighborhood surveys of needs into online maps.

Within two days of the earthquake, a team from the Thomson Reuters Foundation's AlertNet landed a twin-engine plane at Portau-Prince's international airport, hoping to set up an SMS text message-based Emergency Information Service (EIS) to provide free, practical messages to survivors. They lost half their gear and most of their food and water in the landing and tarantulas infested their camp near the runway, but they were undeterred. Working with an innovative humanitarian technology NGO called InSTEDD, the EIS team sent out free, useful Creole language SMS alerts over the same 4636 short code. Twenty-six thousand people subscribed.

The technology provided an easy means for most Haitians to ask for critical help, but the same short code was also being used for general public health messaging causing many subscribers to complain that they reached out in need, only to receive "wash your hands"-type generic messages in response. Tragically, the confusion limited the effectiveness of the experimental short code. In the future, separate numbers will have to be used for outgoing and incoming messages.

Crowd mapping in Haiti proved its enormous potential in responding to humanitarian emergencies; unfortunately, however, relief organizations were not prepared to respond to the thousands of requests for help that came in. Without effective coordination with most of the relief agencies, the actionable data was relatively limited. Nevertheless, it was a remarkable achievement, an unprecedented mobilization of technologists and volunteers. When text messaging was combined with the power of radio, the effects were greatly multiplied. Most important, it represented the first large-scale opportunity for citizens to participate in their own relief and opened a dialogue between the affected communities and service providers. "Many organizations involved in disaster response have, with uneven results, tried to insure affected communities have an important say in their own relief and recovery," said Quintanilla. But Haiti represented "the first-ever humanitarian operation where a collective, multi-agency initiative focused on dialogue with those most affected and enhanced how humanitarians talk and listen to populations affected by disasters." Without this local participation, communities cannot help inform or guide relief services where they are most needed. "Ultimately," reflected Quintanilla, "they are left further disempowered at a time when it is most criti-cal they be heard."

Despite the Herculean efforts of thousands of volunteers, the overall UN emergency response system in Haiti was simply not organized to integrate intelligence from survivors or community leaders, creating a "communications disconnect" between Haitians and emergency response organizations, according to an evaluation by the United States Institute of Peace.

Although the tools for interactivity and dialogue between relief organizations and affected populations now readily exist and the spread of mobile phones is near universal, there has yet to be a paradigm shift by the humanitarian organizations to listen to the people in crisis. As Reed Lindsay reported for *The Nation* on March 11, 2010, "International aid groups compare notes and discuss strategies for distributing aid at 'cluster meetings,' from which ordinary Haitians are in effect banned."

The lack of credible local information became especially apparent as security concerns often delayed aid deliveries. There were several documented instances where international media got out to communities faster than relief organizations and gave sensationalized reports of dangers from local gangs and mobs. "These reports of violence on the streets of Port-au-Prince have been grossly exaggerated and have become a major obstacle to mounting the response needed to save tens of thousands of lives each day," cautioned the American Civil Liberties Union in January 2010. A food drop planned for the seaside town of Leogane, for example, was cancelled after the international media reported violence there. But Roland St. Fort, a community leader there, blogged, "I don't know what security they need to establish. There have been no riots here. The people have been very disciplined. They set up their own security around their outdoor camps." Had the relief organizations had a system in place to converse with the affected populations, these critical delays may have been avoided. It was a missed opportunity.

There are a number of lessons humanitarian organizations can draw from the response to the earthquake in Haiti. As mentioned, local radio remains the most effective means to communicate with disaster-affected communities. Virtually everyone in Haiti had access to a radio and transmitters were quickly repaired or replaced. Local journalists, disc jockeys and talk show hosts will continue to be the source of information most people will turn to. Providing them with reliable information is vital. The international community is finally recognizing the importance of local media in emergencies, but far more should be done to support them. Coordination among the different relief organizations—and with media support and online communities—is essential. Digital phone technology affords the opportunity to aggregate vital data that can improve the delivery of aid, but only if relief organizations are prepared in advance to use it. Telecoms worldwide must establish a system of universal SMS short codes for use by the UN for humanitarian emergencies.

"All the technology in the world can't end suffering or bring back the lives of those lost," lamented Frohardt. "When people are in crisis, they are vulnerable and afraid. Information can help them regain some semblance of control over their lives. It's a matter of respect and empowerment. Delivering relief aid is only part of what they need. When we listen to the survivors of a disaster, we help restore their dignity. That's what makes it all worthwhile."

PART III

WE THE MEDIA

BOUAZIZI'S RAGE

Previous chapters have demonstrated how powerful media can be, for better or for worse. It can be used to save lives in a humanitarian disaster, lift people out of poverty, or reduce conflict. Concentrated in the hands of demagogues, media can foment hatred, atrocities, and war. Much depends on the political environment within which media operate, whether it is state-controlled or independent, diverse, and pluralistic. Newer digital technologies open the possibility of a media revolution that can provide an unimaginable increase and sharing of information wealth; but greater access to information and freedom of speech can also expose long-suppressed indignities.

Mohamed Bouazizi was a young Tunisian man living in Sidi Bouzid, a non-descript town of fifty thousand in the center of the country. The main street that cuts through the length of the town used to be called Rue 7 Novembre, in honor of the day that Ben Ali, the dictator who had ruled the country since 1987, came to power. Today locals refer to it as Rue Mohamed Bouazizi. He was only ten when he became the main provider for his family. Every day he would push his wooden cart to the market, load it with fruits and vegetables and walk back a mile and a half to the local souk. He was honest and hardworking, but was often harassed by police officers who confiscated his scales and produce or fined him for running a stall without permission. In June 2010, the police sent a four hundred-dinar ($280) fine to his home—the equivalent of two months' earnings.

Six months later, on December 17, a policewoman named Fedya Hamdi accosted him on the asphalt lot across from the municipal building on Rue 7 Novembre. When Bouazizi refused to turn over his scale, she allegedly slapped him, spit at him and, together with a colleague, wrestled him to the ground and confiscated his produce. Publicly humiliated, the twenty-six-year-old fruit vendor went to the city hall to demand justice, but no one would speak with him. He returned to the square in front of it, poured paint thinner over his body and set himself on fire.

He was not the first to do so. About a dozen other young Tunisian men had committed suicide in a similar manner in the preceding years. What was different this time was that Bouazizi's cousin, Ali Bouazizi, used his cell phone to shoot a video of a peaceful demonstration led by Bouazizi's mother the day of the burning, and then posted it on Facebook. That, by itself, would not have resulted in the Arab Spring. What amplified the story was that Al Jazeera's live satellite television channel, Mubasher, which trawls the Web looking for video from across the Arab world, picked up the report and rebroadcast it to the entire region.

Dignity Before Bread

This is perhaps the most dramatic example to date of the new media reality and how it is shaping world politics at the speed of the Internet. In the decade preceding the Arab Spring, cell phones became ubiquitous throughout Tunisia. Internet access in the country expanded from near zero in 2000 to 30 percent of the population in 2010. Tunis censored the blogosphere more than any country in the region, but by the time of the revolution in early 2011, nearly one in five Tunisians actively used Facebook.

Increasing access to information in a society with little means for political expression or participation is a prescription for protest. One of the few people who predicted trouble in Tunisia and elsewhere was the economist Daniel Kaufmann, who noted that while information access was rising steadily, most democracy indicators, like free elections and lower levels of corruption, were sharply declining. For most Tunisians, for example, corruption was a pervasive daily humiliation. The economy as a whole was growing—the World Economic Forum had ranked Tunisia first in Africa for economic development in 2008/2009—but increasing unemployment choked off opportunities for the swelling ranks of college graduates.

Across the Middle East and North Africa, those with secondary education and above made up 95 percent of unemployed youth, precisely the people also most likely to have access to the Internet. Two-thirds of the population in the region was under the age of thirty, speaking Twitter as well as Arabic.

Tunisia's youth were impatient for change, faulting their parents' generation for accepting the daily indignities of a dictatorship that was particularly insulting. A slogan shouted over and over again at the demonstration in Sidi Bouzid following Mohamed Bouazizi's self-immolation was "Dignity before Bread." Citizens in Tunisia learned that if they expressed any discontentment with the status quo, they would suffer the wrath of the security apparatus. But, as the Duke University economist Timur Kuran remarked, "When the cost of pretending becomes intolerably high . . . sudden and surprising mass protests can erupt."

Soon the riots grew and spread to the nearby towns of Menzel Bouziane and Regueb. The key organizers of the revolts were the Tunisian labor movement. Although the national Tunisian General Labour Union (UGTT) was very conservative and had been tolerated by the Ben Ali regime, the local branch in Sidi Bouzid was militant and drove the demonstrations forward. Despite desperate attempts by the regime to prevent further video reports, Al Jazeera, Al Arabiya, France 24 and other satellite channels continued to broadcast coverage of the spreading protests and three hundred thousand videos posted on YouTube tagged "Sidi Bouzid" were uploaded by the middle of January 2011. Twitter and Facebook and other social media sites became hotbeds of citizen journalism, allowing protesters to communicate with each other on the ground in Tunisia while getting the story out to the rest of the world.

Mohamed Bouazizi remained in critical condition for eighteen days. President Ben Ali finally visited him in the hospital two weeks after his self-immolation, but by then it was too late for both of them. Bouazizi died on January 4, setting off nationwide protests that spread to the capital, and Ben Ali resigned and fled the country just ten days later.

Preparations for Protest

Why, after decades of military dictatorship, did this once-submissive population rise up to confront the power of the state? While conventional wisdom portrays the Tunisian revolt as a spontaneous uprising, years of organizing by a small but determined group of cyber activists prepared the ground for this moment, successfully spreading coverage of the protests to Tunisians as well as to the rest of the world.

Tunisian and Egyptian activists had been sharing ideas and tactics online for several years. In 2008, following labor unrest in both countries, Tunisian bloggers and online activists formed the Progressive Youth of Tunisia, modeled on a new Egyptian organization called the April 6 Youth Movement, which had gained considerable notoriety. The ease of accessing information and communicating greatly reduced the cost of organizing and accelerated the spread of radical ideas throughout the region.

Sami Ben Gharbia is a Tunisian human rights campaigner who in 2004 co-founded Nawaat.org ("the core"), a popular Tunisian blog and online news aggregator that became the information hub of the revolution. "The role of the Internet in the Tunisian revolution, and building the spirit of protest and change," he reflected, "is the work of at least a decade . . . (Tunisian cyber activists are) techsavvy—they know how to use new information technology, they know how to circumvent censorship, they know how to secure their communications channels, and they were ready for the revolution . . . Censorship created a generation that could circumvent it."

A network of bloggers had formed around Nawaat.org and was connected with other online human rights and freedom of information activists through Global Voices, an international community of bloggers that reports on citizen media and human rights from around the world. On November 28, 2010,

Wikileaks released a batch of seventeen classified cables that the whistle-blowing site had uncovered from the US Embassy in Tunis. Nawaat published them an hour later on a new site called TuniLeaks, with a Twitter hashtag @Tunileaks, before the world press could get the story out.

The documents, transmitted between May 2008 and February 2010, revealed torture in secret prisons and massive corruption by relatives of the president, noting fully half of the businesses in Tunisia had blood or marriage ties to "the Family." Most Tunisians were aware of the mafia-like grip Ben Ali's family had on the economic life of the country, and they especially despised the grotesque displays of wealth and corruption by Ben Ali's wife, Leila Trabelsi, and her extended clan. One cable described how they had unabashedly expropriated for themselves a yacht owned by Bruno Roger, the chairman of Lazard Paris. Another described a dinner attended by the US ambassador at the sumptuous mansion of Nesrine Ben Ali el-Materi and Sakher el-Materi, the president's daughter and son-in-law, where the couple fed their pet tiger, Pasha, four chickens a day at a time when most Tunisians could barely afford one a week.

Frantic to prevent further distribution of the cables in Tunisia, the government quickly blocked TuniLeaks.com, but the story was already circulating widely on the Web. The next day the government blocked Gmail, shut down access to Twitter and stopped all Google searches for #Tunileaks. It censored the electronic version of the Lebanese newspaper *Al Akhbar* and other online publications. But it was futile. The whole country was talking about the personal habits of the ruling family and their close circle, fueling anger on the streets as protests continued to grow after Bouazizi's immolation.

Both the regime and its opponents were aware of the protests that had nearly toppled the rule of the Ayatollahs in Iran after fraudulent elections just a year and a half earlier, in June 2009. Twitter, YouTube, Flickr, Facebook, and other online communication tools had helped mobilize massive protests in Tehran and other Iranian cities, and greatly expanded coverage of the revolt in mainstream media throughout the world. The Iranian government, however, had been much better prepared than its Tunisian counterpart and, apparently, was able to deploy sophisticated technology to selectively jam many of these sites, though a good deal of the blockage might have been the result of excessive traffic. More ominously, the Iranian government may have had the capacity to monitor online conversations to identify leading activists, though again, the actual extent of this is difficult to determine. The US State Department nevertheless took the unprecedented step of asking Twitter to delay scheduled maintenance to avoid disrupting communications among tech-savvy Iranian citizens.

In Tunisia, cyber activists worked around the government's attempts to suppress them, and continued to get the story of the Tunisian revolt out to Arab satellite networks and the Western media without interruption. By providing alternative narratives to the official party line, citizen journalism had delegitimized the power of the state. As Hossam el-Hamalawy, one of the Arab world's most influential bloggers, put it, "In a dictatorship, independent journalism by default becomes a form of activism, and the spread of information is essentially an act of agitation." In a country such as Tunisia, which exerted monopolistic control over the mass media, online eyewitness reports on social media sites prevented the regime from suppressing the news.

There were few foreign media in Tunisia at the time. Al Jazeera and France 24 each had one correspondent on the ground and US media had none, but citizen-generated YouTube videos kept the story alive. Al Jazeera reportedly relied on these videos for 60 percent of its content during the weeks leading up to President Ben Ali's ouster on January 14.

Citizen Journalists

Lina Ben Mhenni, twenty-seven, who blogged in Arabic, English, French, and German under the name "Tunisian Girl," traveled the country clandestinely posting pictures and reports about the street demonstrations and the violent response of the security forces. Her blog became a virtual newsroom for foreign journalists who were not able to see the action themselves.

Mainstream journalists and media analysts find themselves in a quandary over the rise of citizen journalism, which poses threats both economic and professional. It is usually difficult or impossible to verify the accuracy of many of these first-hand accounts, most of which come from advocates and activists who often risk their lives to get their side of the story out. But in the absence of its own reporters, the news media have little choice but to increasingly depend on amateurs. The flood of eyewitness accounts and videos provides a kind of "wisdom of crowds" veracity, while experience over time with particular citizen journalists like Lina Ben Mhenni can establish an individual citizen journalist's credibility.

A key objective of cyber activists everywhere, besides building domestic support, is to influence mainstream media and the Western policy agenda. Courtney Radsch, a researcher of cyber activism in the Arabic-speaking world, wrote, "An increasingly symbiotic relationship between citizen and professional journalism has developed throughout the Arab Spring."

Satellite Television Changes the Game

Mainstream media in the Arab world had been a conservative, even reactionary, factor for decades. But that changed radically with the introduction of satellite news channels. The Egyptian Satellite Channel began transmitting in December 1990, followed a year later by the Middle East Broadcasting Center (MBC). MBC broke the censorship that each national broadcaster in the region had exercised, providing the first transnational news reporting. But it was CNN's international coverage of the 1991 Gulf War which woke up the Arab states to the immense influence of a twenty-four-hour dedicated news channel. In November 1996, after a Saudi-BBC satellite news venture fell apart, Qatar's progressive emir, Sheikh Hamad bin Khalifa Al Thani, saw an opportunity to vastly expand the tiny kingdom's power by launching Al Jazeera, the first twentyfour-hour Arabic all-news channel, with a $140 million investment. Overnight, a little known state on the Persian Gulf with fewer than two million people became a global news superpower.

Not since President Nasser of Egypt used radio to reach the wider Arab audience had there been such a force for pan-Arab nationalism. Nasser invested considerable resources to turn the newly created Sawt al-Arab, *Voice of the Arabs,* into the dominant broadcaster in the Middle East and the principal means for spreading the ideology of the Egyptian revolution of 1952. As Jamal Dajani, the media activist and blogger, wrote,

The Arab nationalism that Egyptian President Gamal Abdel Nasser tried but failed to market to the Arab world in the 1960s has been revived today through satellite TV. The breadth of the coverage has only highlighted the commonalities that exist among the different populations, whether they are living in Marrakesh or Beirut. Arabs throughout the region watch the same sitcoms, see the same religious shows, laugh at the same jokes and cry when they see the same news stories. Their freedoms of information and expression are no longer restricted by their ministries of information or by borders. Democracy might not be a reality on the ground in the Arab world, but pluralism is in the air . . . on satellite TV.

Unlike the radio that propelled Nasserism, the searing emotional messages television can convey provide images that may more easily ignite the "Arab Street." "The Al Jazeera Effect" was a jolting "psychotechtonic shift" for sclerotic and autocratic regimes throughout the Middle East—the apotheosis of "soft power." After Al Jazeera, it would prove impossible to isolate Arab populations from the outside world. Today, more than eight hundred Arab satellite channels compete for audience share with Al Jazeera and its major competitor, Al Arabiya. National borders and the military forces that defend them are less salient protectors of a country's sovereignty in the face of these transnational satellite television channels.

News over satellite television channels that Arab governments were powerless to censor challenged the legitimacy of the state, which had been largely sustained through its monopoly control over the media. There now existed an alternative political narrative to the propaganda of the ruling regimes. It can be argued that such alternative

194

narratives existed before the advent of satellite television and that the "Arab Street" was already dubious of the government's party line. But seeing is truly believing, and knowing that others throughout the region were watching the same images lent an incontrovertible truth to the new coverage. Governments ignored this at their peril. As Mohammed Jassim Al Ali, former managing director of Al Jazeera, said in 2008, "Democracy is coming to the Middle East because of the communications revolution. You can no longer hide information and must now tell people the truth. If you don't, the people won't follow you, they won't support you, they won't obey you."

The Facebook Effect

Karl Marx once wrote, "Shame is a kind of anger which is turned inward. And if a whole nation really experienced a sense of shame, it would be like a lion, crouching ready to spring." The Internet, social media, and satellite television combined to turn Mohamed Bouazizi's private humiliation into a national and then a regional shame. It was a perfect political storm. What began with one distraught fruit vendor in Tunisia struck a chord with many other Arab populations also suffering from autocratic rule. Grievances may have varied from country to country, though youth unemployment was a common factor; nevertheless, people throughout the region experienced the same daily indignities of living in police states, with few opportunities and little freedom of expression.

The media revolution meant images of revolt could be captured, transmitted online and distributed over satellite television to people who spoke a common language and a shared sense of disempowerment. Technology by itself does not cause revolutions—people do. Individual cyber activists in Tunisia had prepared themselves to make the best use of these tools to mobilize the masses, counter government propaganda and censorship, and delegitimize the regime. It was not a "Facebook revolution" per se, but Facebook was the perfect tool for the moment.

Facebook was important, first and foremost, because the Tunisian Internet police, by blocking all other Websites, pushed a critical mass of online activity onto Facebook. In 2007, the government had shuttered YouTube and Daily Motion, another very popular video-sharing Website, and in 2010 closed down Blip TV, Vimeo, Flickr, and others. (When the government tried to block Facebook in 2008, a wave of anti-censorship sentiment forced it to back down.) Certainly not all of these young Netizens were political activists; but by herding all online activity to one platform, the regime inadvertently created an angry and cohesive user community opposed to government censorship. Ethan Zuckerman, the media scholar and Internet guru, calls this the "Cute Cat Theory of Digital Activism," when governments block Websites that are popular for sharing funny pictures and videos only to turn a small percentage of users into anti-censorship activists. The state can shut down online platforms specifically designed for political dissent without great risk, but more mundane sites are harder to censor without radicalizing a larger group of otherwise apolitical actors.

As a closed system confined to one's personal social network, Facebook has certain advantages over blogs. The blogosphere is usually dominated by a few established bloggers. Most readers will gravitate to the most popular sites; it becomes harder for new voices to establish critical mass. But social media sites like Facebook, and also Twitter, provide a more personal and egalitarian platform. Small audiences that begin there can multiply rapidly through network connections.

Social Media Matters

Just before the Arab Spring erupted in Sidi Bouazid, there was a fierce debate in the Western press about social media's value in mobilizing political dissent, centered around a provocative article by Malcolm Gladwell in the October 4, 2010 issue of the *New Yorker* titled "Small Change: Why the Revolution Will Not Be Tweeted."

Gladwell mocked "cyber utopians" for exaggerating the power of social networks. "The world, we are told, is in the midst of a revolution," said Gladwell, sarcastically. "The new tools of social media have reinvented social activism. With Facebook and Twitter and the like, the traditional relationship between political authority and popular will has been upended, making it easier for the powerless to collaborate, coordinate and give voice to their concerns." But Gladwell would have none of it.

He went on to ridicule "digital evangelists" like Clay Shirky, author of *Here Comes Everybody,* for overstating the impact of social media on the new wave of political activism. To put things in perspective, Gladwell contrasted the courageous "high-risk activism" of the students who staged the first sit-in at the lunch counter at Woolworth's in downtown Greensboro, North Carolina with the sometimes large but inconsequential, low-risk involvement typical of virally spread, online political campaigns. "We seem to have forgotten what activism is," wrote Gladwell.

Quoting the Stanford sociologist Doug McAdam, Gladwell concluded that high-risk activism is a "strong-tie" phenomenon, whereas platforms of social media are built around "weak ties." Online campaigns can attract many people to sign up "by not asking too much of them," opined Gladwell. McAdam's study of Mississippi Freedom Summer demonstrated that the most important factor in commitment was the strong, personal ties activists had with their closest friends. Social media, by contrast, grouped superficial acquaintances who shared in each other's frivolities, according to Gladwell.

The other crucial distinction between traditional activism and its online variant is that social media lacked hierarchical organization. "When taking on a powerful and organized establishment," Gladwell declared, "you have to be a hierarchy." Finally, he concluded his jeremiad by belittling Shirky and other cyber activists. "The instruments of social media are well suited to making the existing social order more efficient. They are not a natural enemy of the status quo."

The events in Tunisia and later in Egypt would bury Gladwell's righteous indignation with historical scorn. Not only would social media prove its mettle in mobilizing the masses, "collaborating, coordinating and giving voice to their concerns," but also, as we shall see, its very lack of hierarchy was arguably its greatest strength in confronting and overthrowing the regime. The revolution in Tunisia was certainly no low-risk adventure. And, apparently, the personal ties in the social media matrix were strong enough to validate and sustain oppositional protest. Chrystia Freeland, a columnist for the *Financial Times*, calls this the "Groupon effect." "The combination of satellite television and social networking," she wrote, "has made it dramatically easier for the disaffected to overcome one of the central obstacles to organizing regime change—letting each individual know what views are shared by enough people to make protesting worthwhile, and relatively safe."

For many, from citizens who could see the protests from their windows to editors in foreign capitals trying to figure out the story, social media specialists became clearing houses for fresh information—often confirming what was true and debunking hoaxes, rumors and lies. One of the leaders of the social media movement was Andy Carvin, a senior strategist for National Public Radio (NPR), a national US radio network. From his office and his home in Washington, DC, Carvin sometimes found himself at the center of the coverage. He scoured the social media sites, first for the uprising in Tunisia and then throughout the other Arab Spring countries, passing along news from tweets and blogs and postings and sharing photos and videos. Soon major news organizations were keeping an eye on his Twitter feed for the latest news, and particularly for confirming facts and refuting rumors. Carvin, who described himself as a war correspondent who didn't attend the war, chronicled his role in his 2013 book *Distant Witness: Social Media, the Arab Spring and a Journalism Revolution*.

Several journalists and commentators, writing after the Tunisian uprising, saw in the revolt evidence of social media's continuing power to confront authoritarian regimes, a pattern that followed Ukraine's 2004 Orange Revolution, Iran's Green Movement, and Moldova's so-called "Grape Revolution" in April 2009. The Internet critic Evgeny Morozov effectively changed the name of the latter to the "Twitter Revolution." In addition, he pointed out that democracy activists in Ukraine's Orange Revolution had effectively used cell phones and texting to mobilize crowds of demonstrators; but in Moldova's capital, Chisinau, protesters relied more on Twitter.

Other commentators scoffed at Morozov's analysis, noting how very few Twitter accounts existed in the country. But Morozov was unfazed.

> *People who point to the low number of Twitter users in Moldova as proof of the mythical nature of the subject have conceptual difficulties understanding how networks work. . . . On a good network, you don't need to have the maximum number of connections to be powerful—you just need to be connected to enough nodes with connections of their own . . . The fact that so few (Twitter users) actually managed to keep the entire global Twitter-sphere discussing an obscure country for almost a week only proves that Twitter has more power than we think.*

While there has been an evolution of technological tools that political organizers have used with increasing effectiveness—from email and blogs to SMS text messaging, Twitter, and Facebook—the blogosphere, in fact, is a rich tapestry of interconnected messaging systems that complement and amplify one another. Cyber enthusiasts sometimes err by making a fetish out of the latest online applications. They are simply apolitical tools, however powerful, that can be used by anyone. But in the hands of skilled activists, they can tap into latent social grievances and turn into virtual viruses of revolutionary anger, as was the case in Egypt just a month after Ben Ali fled his capital in Tunisia.

THE ROAD TO
TAHRIR SQUARE

There were many factors converging to ignite revolt in
Tunisia and Egypt in 2011. Aging dictators, whose decades-
long rule had bred endemic corruption, dominated both
countries. In living memory, none of their citizens had
ever voted in a free election. Economic inequality was
conspicuous. But poverty alone was not a sufficient cause
of the revolt that continues to shake the region. Nor was
it the lack of democracy in the formal sense. Rather, it
was the injustices of everyday life, the lack of opportunity
and the humiliations from arbitrary authorities that led to
revolution.

Egypt, like Tunisia, had a bulging youth population,
digital natives adept at using social media, with high rates
of secondary education but very few job opportunities.
It is hard to overestimate the frustration and anxiety this
caused, as young men were forced to delay marriage in
a society where premarital sex was prohibited. In 2002,
hoping to jump start Egypt's economy, President Hosni
Mubarak appointed Ahmed Nazif, a young professor
from the faculty of engineering at Cairo University, to
be his new minister of communications and information
technology. Nazif proceeded to establish free Internet
connectivity and access to low cost computers sold by

the government through the Egyptian Telecommunications Company. Internet use shot up and fifty million Egyptians bought cell phones, many embedded with a Facebook mobile Web application. Just two months after free Internet was introduced, Mubarak promoted the young professor to be his new prime minister.

Soon, however, just as in Tunisia, Egyptian cyber activists learned to use these social media tools to mobilize the masses, leading to the Egyptian revolution of January 25 to February 14, 2011. Caught in "the dictator's dilemma," Mubarak had tried to reap the benefits of globalization and the communications revolution; instead, he unleashed the forces of his own destruction. "There is a techie, passionate, frustrated generation now on the playground," warned the blogger Nora Younis.

But in Egypt, as elsewhere, the seeds of revolt were years in the making, especially among members of banned groups like the Muslim Brotherhood and unofficial labor unions. The decades-long emergency law that President Mubarak initiated upon his ascension to power allowed the military government to arrest and detain without charge, to limit public gatherings and to operate a special security court. This effectively eliminated a public space for political agitation, a vacuum that the Internet and social media would fully exploit. Egyptians had grown adept at expressing their discontent through cartoons and satire in the largely constricted mainstream media in the years leading up to the revolution, but it was only in virtual space that large numbers of citizens could more or less openly express their contempt for the system.

In 2004, online activists formed a new political movement called "Kefaya" (Enough), whose central message was aimed at reforming the presidential system in an attempt to block the transfer of power to Hosni Mubarak's son, Gamal. Active during the 2005 constitutional referendum and presidential election campaigns, it subsequently lost momentum, suffering from internal dissent, leadership change, and a more general frustration at the apparent inability of Egypt's political opposition to confront the regime. But it did achieve a notable success as the first movement to openly oppose the dictator.

April 6 Youth

Ahmed Maher was twenty-five when he joined Kefaya. Exceedingly quiet, Maher is known as a thoughtful political strategist. "To spend an afternoon, or even a few days, with Maher is to watch him listening," wrote David Wolman in *The Instigators*. A reluctant leader, Maher is not a charismatic speaker. But people follow him because of his bravery and sincerity. The Egyptian blogger Wael Abbas told Wolman that Maher "is a velvet fist in a velvet glove."

An obsessive reader, Maher got hold of his first computer in 1998 when he went to college and began frequenting cybercafés to play online games. He read political blogs and eventually joined Kefaya, getting arrested in April 2006 during a sit-in supporting a group of judges who were calling for a more independent judiciary. He spent two months in prison.

The following winter, Egypt's national soccer team reached the finals of the Africa Cup and forty-five thousand people "friended" its Facebook fan page. Maher and his Kefaya cohorts instantly realized the potential of social media for political organizing. Frustrated that the old oppositional political parties were unwilling to stand up to the regime, Maher, a civil engineer by training, had been searching for new ways to build a movement.

In Egypt, as in Tunisia, organized labor's support for student protests helped turned the tide against the old regimes. Although Ben Ali tolerated an organized trade union movement in Tunisia and Mubarak did not—property tax collectors succeeded in establishing the first independent union in Egypt in half a century only a few years earlier—in both countries' revolutions, labor proved decisive. "December 2006 was definitely the turning point that will be engraved forever as the start of the liberation of Egypt," wrote Hossam El-Hamalawy, an influential Egyptian journalist and blogger. That was when Wedad Dermerdash, a forty-four-year-old mother of four, led a strike for higher pay and to protest the soaring price of chicken in el-Mahallah el-Kubra, a crumbling cotton mill town in the Nile River Delta that housed the largest factory in Egypt. She printed leaflets and pushed her fellow workers to walk out. At first, only the women joined her. Through the windows they could see the men, standing by their machines, afraid. Taunted by the women, the men finally found their courage and for three days the workers occupied the factory grounds. On the fourth day, management caved. The victory at Mahallah encouraged militants throughout the country.

In the spring of 2008, hoping to organize wider support for the growing labor unrest that followed in the wake of the Mahallah victory, Maher joined with Israa Abdel-Fattah, a twenty-seven-year-old human resources coordinator, to mobilize young activists in cyberspace. With a new strike being planned at Mahallah on April 6, Maher and Abdel-Fattah created the April 6 Youth (A6Y) Facebook page and called for a general strike in solidarity with the workers. She had never even taken part in a demonstration until then. They launched the April 6 Youth group on March 23, using their real names for their Facebook profiles, and invited three hundred of their friends to join them. The page went viral along with thousands of Tweets. By the next morning, three thousand people had signed up; in two weeks it had sixty thousand members. Even Twitter co-founder Biz Stone was amazed. "When we heard about this story and that Twitter was being used in Egypt in 2008 to organize these protests, that was one of the early eye-opening experiences for us, that made us realize this was not just something in the Bay Area for, you know, technical geeks to fool around with . . . but a global-communications system that could be used for almost anything and everything," he recalled.

Few people joined the general strike on April 6, but the sit-in at Mahallah turned into a violent street riot as security forces attacked demonstrators with tear gas and rubber bullets. At least four people were killed. Video of the police assaults ricocheted around the blogosphere and over satellite television on Al Jazeera, dominating the news in Egypt for a week. Maher went underground, but the police pulled Israa Abdel-Fattah out of a Cairo café on the morning of the strike and arrested her under the notorious Emergency Law by which authorities can hold citizens without charge. "Facebook Girl," as she became known, was an instant online heroine. If the authorities were not anxious about the potential of social media to spark a revolt among the country's youth before, they paid attention now.

The April 6 Youth movement gained quite a bit of notoriety in Egypt, especially among the online cognoscenti. Maher and his cohorts tried to hold a follow-up rally in May in downtown Cairo, but this time the police were prepared. The authorities ordered telecoms not to connect calls between anonymous subscribers, preventing communication between activists who routinely switched their SIM cards to hide their identities. The regime also temporarily raised wages, hoping to head off the kind of grievances that had fueled the riots in Mahallah.

Maher avoided arrest at the demonstration; but three days later as he was driving to work in his run-down Fiat, police officers surrounded his car, pulled him out, handcuffed him, and drove him to the New Cairo police station. He was transferred to a state security facility at Lazoghly and tortured for thirty-six hours. Agents stripped him and covered him with oil to prevent the visible signs of blows, dragged him across the floor and threatened him with electrocution and rape. When he was released he went to his parents' house. He would have preferred to stay in his own apartment, but it was his mother's birthday and she was sick with cancer. "Are you OK?" she asked him, noticing a turtleneck sweater he was wearing to hide bruises. "Yes, I just slept funny," he told her.

"Maher's aura of decency," wrote David Wolman, "coupled with his regular-guy street cred, only increased after he was tortured, drawing more young people into A6Y." The April 6 Youth movement struck a chord among the growing legion of young Egyptians active in cyberspace and offered a narrow bridge between Cairo's elite and the working class. The number of Internet users had jumped from 1.5 million in 2004 to more than 13.6 million by 2008. Facebook use in Egypt exploded following the April 6 strikes. By the end of 2010, Egypt had nearly 4 million users. Youth between the ages of fifteen and twenty-nine made up about 70 percent of Facebook users in the Arab region and online discussions about political tactics streamed across borders. Clay Shirky made an important observation when he noted that "access to information is far less important, politically, than access to conversation." The increasingly radicalized young cyber activists realized, however, that to succeed they would have to "connect the revolution of freedom with the revolution of bread," as April 6th organizers put it. The rhetoric of reform from the Kefaya period was turning into a broader call for revolutionary change.

When the massive street demonstrations erupted in Iran to protest fraudulent elections in June 2009, the specter of digitally organized revolts haunted autocratic rulers throughout the Middle East. A great deal of the news coverage focused on the Iranian regime's sophisticated suppression of Facebook, Twitter, Flickr, and other online tools, along with the opposition's resilience in circumventing the blockages. But there were also disturbing reports that the security services were using online surveillance to identify and track protest organizers and activists.

When the Green Movement in Iran was finally crushed by brute force in August 2009, online activists in Egypt and Tunisia took stock. They studied what worked and took note of the glaring weaknesses of the Iranian grassroots opposition movement. Soliciting suggestions online, they created a manual on protest methods and did a post-mortem analysis of cyber security failures. Digital media experts in the April 6 movement contacted Italian anarchist party activists for advice on how to use "ghost servers," which bounce Internet searches to non-existent servers to confuse security forces. Ramy Raoof, twenty-four, an online media expert for Global Voices and the Egyptian Initiative for Personal Rights, created a digital tool for using mobile phones and Twitter to secure immediate legal help for arrested activists. He also offered advice on how to use international phone lines to send text messages during government-imposed SMS text shutdowns.

Maher, arrested four times by the time of the Iranian protests, began a serious study of the history and tactics of non-violent movements around the world. He and other April 6 leaders took a crash course online to learn about the US civil rights movement, read the writings of Gandhi, and connected with the organizers of Serbia's Otpor! student movement, whose logo of a clenched fist they had already adopted as their own. In October 2000, Otpor! led the movement that overthrew the government of Slobodan Milosevic, using adroit applications of nonviolent protest strategies and tactics learned from an American organizer named Gene Sharp. After the rise and fall of the Green Movement in Iran in 2009, several A6Y organizers flew to Belgrade for training.

In addition to learning how to use new digital tools to organize protests, cyber activists sought to make the most effective use of new media technologies to get their message out. Bassem Samir, the director of the Egyptian Democratic Academy, an election-monitoring group affiliated with the April 6 movement, was a popular source for English-speaking journalists. Watching the jerky, poorly shot videos taken during the Green Revolution in Iran, Samir thought the images were too confusing to be as compelling as they might have been. He accepted an offer from Witness, an American nongovernmental organization, to bring a delegation of Egyptians to the United States to get trained by professional digital journalists and documentary filmmakers. Then, in the run-up to the parliamentary elections in Egypt in 2010, Samir brought a group of American journalists to Egypt to train April 6 organizers in digital media skills.

One of the trainers was Maryam Ishani, a conflict journalist who had worked for the United Nations. "They were trained on how to convey their content out of the event site safely: running exercises where photographers would hand off small memory flash cards at frequent intervals, switch cameras with activists who would pose as innocent bystanders, and send in camera teams in waves instead of all at once," she recounted. "Another novel tactic was carrying a decoy memory card with photos of tourist sites on it to hand over to police," she recalled. After showing an iconic image of a Sandinista throwing a Molotov cocktail, one of the other trainers displayed the image of a crowd in Tehran standing over the body of Neda Agha-Soltan, all holding cell phones. The video of the shooting death of the twenty-six-year-old, as she stood observing the election protests, had become the iconic symbol of the regime's oppression. "Your camera phone is now your Molotov cocktail," the trainer told the young photojournalists.

At the end of a session on personal security practices, Samir told Maryam Ishani, "They need to stop thinking of revolution as martyrdom. They are so used to thinking that if they don't get arrested or beaten up they aren't committed enough." This was not going to be their fathers' revolution.

The protest strategies and tactics they learned would prove essential when they finally confronted the Egyptian security state. Clever as these might be, however, they work only on the presumption that the population has reached a point of no return and are willing to risk injury, arrest, or torture by taking to the streets.

We Are All Khaled Said

If there was a tipping point in Egypt's popular revolution, it probably was the brutal death of Khaled Mohamed Said at the hands of two secret police officers in Alexandria on June 6, 2010. A photograph of his disfigured face—his lower lip ripped in half, teeth missing, his jaw dislocated—lying in a pool of blood, was posted on the Facebook page of the former opposition presidential candidate Ayman Nour, who was still in jail after daring to challenge Hosni Mubarak in the 2005 election. The victim, twenty-eight years old, had been dragged out of a cybercafé and beaten to death in broad daylight in front of a group of pedestrians. The impunity of the attack and the biography that emerged of the young man, who loved music and studied computer programming, struck a nerve among young, wired Egyptians. Like the self-immolation of Mohamed Bouazizi in Tunisia, the murder of Khaled Mohamed Said turned an individual humiliation into collective anger.

When another young Egyptian programmer, Wael Ghonim, saw the gruesome photograph of Khaled Said that a friend had posted on Ghonim's Facebook wall, he began to cry uncontrollably. The thirty-year-old Ghonim was no radical. However, he was a savvy Facebook user, and realized that a Facebook page was far more effective in spreading information than a Facebook group. As soon as someone "likes" a page, Facebook treats the person and the page as a "friend," so posts automatically appear on one's wall, making it easier for posts to go viral.

"A real-life introvert, yet an Internet extrovert," as Ghonim described himself, he was fairly in love with computers. As a college freshman, he created a Website called IslamWay.com to help Muslims network with one another. However moderate it may have been, such a Website might invite a strong response from Egypt's State Security; consequently, Ghonim administered the site anonymously. IslamWay soon became one of the most popular Islamic destinations on the Internet. An English version spread rapidly among non-Arab-speaking Muslims on the Web.

It was there that Ghonim met his future wife, Ilka, an American who had recently converted to Islam. He loved America, most especially because of its freedom of religion, but his heart remained in Egypt. His real goal in life eluded him—to work for Google. After enormous success helping to launch Mubasher.info, an Arabic version of Reuters and Bloomberg, Ghonim finally landed a position with Google and moved with his family to Dubai.

Sitting in his comfortable apartment, confronted by the harrowing picture of Khaled Said, Ghonim felt compelled to act. He knew he had all the skills needed to publicize the killing. Browsing the Web, he discovered a page had already been launched under the title "My Name Is Khaled Mohamed Said;" but although it had attracted tens of thousands of followers, its tone was too radical for Ghonim's tastes. He wanted a page that was more emotional and less ideological, one that would attract the widest possible audience. He would write in the colloquial Egyptian dialect rather than classical Arabic and would address his readers in the first person. *Kullena Khaled Said* (*We Are All Khaled Said*) was launched with a simple post. "Today they killed Khaled. If I don't act for his sake, tomorrow they will kill me." Within two minutes, three hundred members had friended the page; within an hour, there were three thousand. Ghonim avoided identifying the page with any organization or political party, making it more accessible to the general public. At the end of the first day, *Kullena Khaled Said* had made thirty-six thousand friends.

Ghonim had caught a tiger by the tail, but as the administrator of the Facebook page, he was as much facilitator as leader. For security reasons, but also because he feared becoming a public figure, Ghonim maintained anonymity as the administrator. As details and eyewitness accounts of the brutal murder of Khaled Said began to emerge, several prominent politicians publicly condemned the killing. The official police account alleged he had tried to swallow a pack of marijuana, choked and died while officers tried to extract it. But another account came from the young man's mother, who told the independent newspaper *AlShorouk* that her son was murdered for possessing a video showing local police dividing up confiscated drugs and money. Soon the video, allegedly found on Khaled's cell phone, circulated widely on the Internet.

Ghonim posted the date and place of Khaled's funeral along with videos of various other acts of torture by members of the police force. He urged people to attend, and a thousand showed up. Within three months, *We Are All Khaled Said* had 250,000 friends, larger than many mainstream media operations. The April 6 Youth Movement called for a demonstration against police brutality in Cairo in front of the Ministry of the Interior on June 25, 2010. By this time Ghonim was working closely with Maher and other leaders of the April 6 Youth Movement via Gmail from Dubai, though even they did not know his real identity. As the anonymous administrator of *We Are All Khaled Said,* Ghonim had become a powerful player in the burgeoning online political sphere.

The A6Y demonstration fizzled out when a massive police

presence surrounded the protesters. Shortly afterward, however, a book called *The Road to the Presidential Palace* suggested that if one hundred thousand citizens gathered in Tahrir Square, they could make a revolution. But there was not yet the critical mass needed to overwhelm the security forces, and although activists might dream of the day, no one seriously imagined it. A different strategy would have to be employed to gradually build a mass movement.

A Facebook user named Mohamed from Alexandria posted a suggestion. "How about if we all gather along the Alexandria coast on Friday? We would face the sea with our backs to the street holding hands in silent expression of our disapproval of the injustice inflicted upon Khaled Said. . . . It's not a demonstration, but a silent expression of disapproval." An hour after Mohamed made his suggestion, Ghonim created a Facebook "event" called "A Silent Stand of Prayer for the Martyr Khaled Said Along the Alexandria Corniche." It would take place in just two days on Friday, August 20, 2010.

Ideas soon poured in. There would be no signs, no chants, no political leaflets. Participants were urged to wear black. Many of the more experienced militants ridiculed the idea, but others called for similar "silent stands" in Cairo and other cities. Ghonim worked around the clock promoting the concept and in two days the Facebook event attracted one hundred thousand followers. Khaled Said's mother agreed to attend. The international media were alerted.

On the afternoon of the demonstration, though, shortly before five o'clock, security forces were spread along the Corniche. For a time, Ghonim, glued to his computer in Dubai, was heartbroken, afraid this first call to action would result in even greater despair. Then an activist on Twitter reported that more than a hundred people were lined up along the Corniche in the Cleopatra District in Alexandria, all wearing black and quietly reading the Quran or the Bible. Ghonim prayed that others would join them, knowing Egyptians are notoriously late because of traffic congestion. Soon they did, and pictures of the peaceful protesters clad in black flew around the blogosphere. A video taken by a Facebook page member from Alexandria, as she drove by slowly in her car, lasted a full five minutes. Reuters reported that eight thousand people took part in the Silent Stand, likely an inflated number. That a Facebook page unaffiliated with any organized party or movement could mobilize people was a clear demonstration that the virtual world could spill over into the real. For Ghonim the great success of an otherwise modest protest was that most of the Silent Stand's participants were young men and women who had never taken part in anything like it before. They had "broken the fear barrier," he wrote.

Writing to Maher under the alias "Khaled Said after the Silent Stand," Ghonim sought to bridge any divide between his non-political approach and the sophisticated street smart organizers of the April 6 Youth Movement. "You and *Kefaya* were the first people in Egypt to wake up and hopefully, God willing, this awakening will continue and we can do something to change this country because we all have the same goal," he began.

Maher responded immediately to this anonymous interlocutor who had brought together a quarter-of-a-million friends to a site protesting police brutality. He praised "Said" for his mobilizing efforts and offered to make a declaration between the two groups "to consult, collaborate, and coordinate together."

"Said" replied excitedly at 3:13 a.m.: "I can't begin to describe how happy I was when I read your e-mail."

At the end of the year, wondering what action to organize to build upon the momentum of the Silent Stand, Khaled Abdel Rahman Mansour, an undergraduate in journalism at Mansoura University, suggested a demonstration of some kind to coincide with National Police Day on January 25, an annual event to commemorate fifty Egyptian police officers killed by the British in 1952. Ghonim had made Mansour, twenty-four, the co-administrator of the *We Are All Khaled Said* page to cover for him when he traveled. "Said" wrote to Maher: "January 25th is 'Police Day.' We want to celebrate it."

Maher responded, "Cool. We celebrated it last year." But the 2009 demonstration had been busted before it could begin.

"Said" thought he could help build greater support this time through his network. They agreed that *We Are All Khaled Said* would endorse and advertise a January 25 event while Maher and A6Y would coordinate the logistics. As they began to develop popular support around the call for demonstrations on Police Day, a political earthquake shook the Arab world: on January 14 Ben Ali resigned the presidency of Tunisia and fled the country with his wife.

January 25th

In Egypt, the fall of an Arab dictator before a popular revolution was electrifying. January 25 now had a much greater significance than a protest against police brutality. Hesitantly, but compelled by the events in Tunisia, Ghonim changed the name of his Facebook event from "Celebrating Egyptian Police Day—January 25" to "January 25: Revolution Against Torture,

215

Poverty, Corruption, and Unemployment." It was "game on!"

Egypt's official media desperately played down the events in Tunis, but the Internet was aflame with articles and opinions. Five Egyptian young men tried to self-immolate like Bouazizi. Other Facebook pages and many organizations began to support the January 25 page, which had jumped to five hundred thousand friends two days after it was launched. Only the Muslim Brotherhood conspicuously refused to participate, saying, "We cannot tie our parties and entities to a virtual world," though many of its younger members and a few key leaders participated as individuals.

A week before the protests, a twenty-six-year-old veiled woman named Asmaa Mahfouz, looking straight into the camera, posted a YouTube video challenging Egyptian men. "Sitting at home following us on the news and on Facebook only leads to our humiliation," she pleaded. "It leads to *my* humiliation. If you have honor and dignity as a man, then come out. Come out and protect me and the other girls at the protest. If you stay at home, you deserve everything that happens to you. And you will be guilty before your nation and your people." Her exhortation flashed virally through the blogosphere.

As the twenty-fifth approached, one hundred thousand Facebook friends committed to take to the streets. Ghonim reached out to the Ultras, the xenophobic soccer fans who had clashed previously with the police, and who would later play an important role in defending Tahrir Square. While Ghonim built mass support for the January 25 protests, Maher and his April 6 cohort prepared for the coming confrontation. They decided to have different opposition groups take responsibility for different parts of the city, organizing marches that would converge on Tahrir Square. None of them would carry banners associated with political parties—only the Egyptian flag. The demands were for higher wages, the resignation of the hated interior minister Habib el-Adley and an end to the notorious Emergency Law giving free reign to the security forces to imprison anyone they wanted. The A6Y group flooded the Internet with guides to non-violent tactics that they took straight out of the playbook of the 2003 Yugoslavian revolution.

Maher and Ghonim were in constant contact, though Maher still did not know the identity of this anonymous Webmaster. Just five days after announcing the January 25 protests and six days before the demonstrations were to start, Wael Ghonim spoke at an Al Jazeera-sponsored conference in Qatar. Ahmed Maher and Israa Abdel-Fattah, the founders of the April 6 Youth Movement, were there as well. Without revealing his other identity, Ghonim, who participated as a Google manager and not as an activist, spoke with Maher and Abdel-Fattah at lunch about the coming protests and asked if locations had been determined. Israa responded that the *"Kullena Khaled Said"* administrator was coordinating with political activists and that locations would be announced soon. After lunch, Ghonim sat in a corner where he could still see Maher and sent him a message to discuss locations. It was a surreal moment as he watched Maher reply to him on his cell phone.

On the night of January 22, as Ghonim prepared to leave for Cairo on the 4 a.m. flight out of Dubai, he wrote to Nadine Wahab, a US-based Egyptian human rights activist he had chosen as the official administrator of *"Kullena Khaled Said"* after Facebook threatened to close the site because it was managed by fake accounts. He instructed her to wait a week before announcing his relationship to *"Kullena Khaled Said,"* in the event that he was arrested. He also made arrangements for the site to be continually updated, if he were taken into custody.

At 11:30 a.m. on the twenty-fifth, Maher drove past the front of Mostafa Mahmoud Mosque, one of the four major gathering points chosen for the marches on Tahrir Square. It was teeming with riot police, but few if any demonstrators. Maher had anticipated this and had dispatched eight groups of twenty A6Y veterans to different working class neighborhoods surrounding the mosque. His team had carefully studied Google Maps to sketch out the best routes.

An hour later the call went out to each of the coordinators with the locations for where to begin. Chanting "Long Live Egypt" and "Bread, Freedom, Human Dignity," they exhorted people to march with them and converge on the area in front of the mosque; from there the group would walk together to Tahrir Square. Even before the official start time of two o'clock, Mostafa Mahmoud Square filled with about seven thousand people who had answered the Facebook calls. The scene was chaotic. People were anxious to move. Maher jumped on top of a fence and yelled, "Just wait! My friends are coming. More people are coming!" and convinced them to sit down. Then on his cell phone he heard from one of his coordinators, "Maher! We have 10,000 people!" From another, "We must be 15,000 people!" From his elevated position Maher looked out over a sea of people converging on the square in front of the mosque. Nothing like this had ever happened in Egypt. The more experienced A6Y organizers created a perimeter around the marchers in the front with locked arms and headed towards Tahrir Square to meet the others coming from the different directions.

After years of effectively blocking protesters with superior numbers, the police were unprepared for the size of the demonstrations. Surging with confidence, the marchers changed their chant to "Al-shaab yureed isqat al-nizam" ("The people demand the fall of the regime"), the signature chant from the Tunisian revolution. As the thousands of protesters converged on Tahrir Square, they celebrated and embraced each other. There were scattered battles with police along the way and much brutality. A thousand demonstrators were arrested. By 3 p.m., spurred by coverage on satellite television channels, protesters occupied half of Tahrir Square while the police began using tear gas, water cannons, and baton charges in a fruitless attempt to clear it. In one of many surreal standoffs, the police began throwing rocks at the protesters. Thousands more demonstrators continued to stream in and reinforce the occupation.

Protesters kept up with what was happening in different parts of the city and in Suez, Alexandria and other parts of Egypt in real time on Twitter. When Facebook and Twitter were shut down temporarily in the square around 4:30 p.m., tech-savvy tweeters instructed people how to use proxy servers to get around the blockage.

No one had really expected the Square to be taken and there were no plans for what to do next. They held on to Tahrir for almost nine hours, but by one in the morning, when the crowds had begun to thin, the police managed to clear the square. Ghonim sent out a message when Facebook was restored, calling for a general strike the next two days, Wednesday and Thursday, January 26 and 27, with a massive rally and return to Tahrir Square after Friday prayers.

With Facebook only intermittently available in Egypt on the night of the twenty-fifth and the next morning, Ghonim prepared an online form to collect email addresses of the page's members. Twenty thousand friends filled it out, but it was a big tactical mistake. By the time the invitation reached more than a million people, reports started coming in that State Security was arresting people on the list, so Ghonim deleted it. He created another Facebook event for January 28 titled "The Day of Rage: A Revolution Against Corruption, Injustice, Torture and Unemployment." That the Muslim Brotherhood had refused to endorse the January 25 march was, in retrospect, one of the great legacies of the demonstration, having proved that the young organizers could mobilize masses of people without the Brotherhood's legendary grassroots machine. Now the "brothers" announced they would join the demonstration, greatly expanding the number of protesters and providing disciplined shock troops to help withstand the assaults against them. It also brought the formidable Brotherhood media operation behind the protesters, exhorting their followers in the mosques, through SMS texts and online to join the revolt.

The next day, one of Ghonim's closest associates, Mostafa alNagar, emailed him to warn that the security forces were desperate to discover the identity of the *Kullena Khaled Said* Facebook page administrator. The police had brutally tortured Mostafa but he never revealed the name, he told Ghonim in a chat session. Relieved, Ghonim nevertheless destroyed the SIM card on his Egyptian cell phone, knowing the police could locate his whereabouts with it.

By the morning of the twenty-seventh, the Facebook event he had created for Friday the twenty-eighth, "The Day of Rage," had already reached a half-million followers. But Facebook, Twitter, and the Internet—all key to mobilizing people and organizing the demonstrations—became far less important once the action moved to the streets.

The Media War

After the twenty-fifth, the role of cyber activists shifted to citizen journalism. Egyptian television and the official media completely ignored the political earthquake of the day before. As violence escalated, professional journalists had trouble reporting from the streets and increasingly relied on photos and first-hand accounts from non-professionals. One site, *Rasd* ("monitoring"), which the mainstream media learned to depend on, collected reports, photos and video uploaded from thousands of protesters across the country. Three hundred and fifty thousand of its members kept up with events through its minute-to-minute updates. The mobile phone gave protesters a tool to actively participate in the narrative that would define the story. But then the most important media became television.

State sovereignty is ultimately a psychological reality, and control over state television is its most potent symbol. Having ruled Egypt for forty years, Mubarak was practically synonymous with the nation itself. As the protests continued to escalate around Tahrir Square, the impact of the demonstrations affected life throughout the capital. Still, most people experienced the violence and the tear gas only on television. State TV continued to project a narrative of normality, barely covering the revolution unfolding on the streets of Cairo. Those who had access to Al Jazeera, Al Arabia or other Arab language satellite channels saw an entirely different description of reality, but Egyptians were used to living with this kind of cognitive dissonance. Outside the capital, most people got their news from the state satellite channel, Nile TV, which alternately ignored the revolt or blamed it on outside forces.

Shahira Amin was a popular newsreader for Nile TV.

Unlike American news anchors, the readers on state television simply read a script written for them by the ministry of the interior. Amin was out of the country for the first five days of the revolution, but followed events as they unfolded on the BBC. When she came home, she was shocked by the deceitful coverage on Nile's news programs. Handed a press release to read on air that claimed "thugs" from the Muslim Brotherhood were responsible for the mayhem, Amin told her bosses, "I'm not reading this. It doesn't make sense." It claimed that five people had died, but that there had been no clashes. "You know," she said, "we are supposed to be telling the world what is happening, just three minutes away from this building."

A few days later she telephoned Mahmoud Wagdy, the new minister of the interior, while live on the air. "What are you going to do?" she asked him. He replied, "I promise change."

Incredulous, she responded, "We've been waiting thirty years and nothing has happened, why should we believe that now?"

The minister was equally incredulous, "Are you sure this is Egyptian television?" Then Amin put down the phone and walked out of the studio. Similar defections took place on television and in the press. The regime lost the last remnants of legitimacy. With alternative sources of news coverage, Mubarak's authority was being challenged as never before.

Desperate to contain the damage from around-the-clock live video images of security forces beating citizens in the heart of the capital, the government ordered a crackdown on the international media. Government-paid enforcers viciously attacked reporters from the major networks and news agencies as well as independent-minded Egyptian journalists. Al Jazeera, which had the most comprehensive coverage and was the go-to channel for news junkies and policymakers around the world, was a particular target. Security forces revoked the network's license, trashed its offices, beat and arrested its journalists, and forced many of them into hiding. Still, the journalists showed enormous courage, as much as any of the demonstrators, in getting the story out. For example, an Al Jazeera cameraman trying to film from the square on the twenty-fifth was struck by eleven rubber bullets. In the face of this unprecedented assault on the world press, the media had become an active participant in the making of history. Though they struggled to maintain their professional impartiality, reporters staying on the air became as important to the revolution as protesters staying on the streets.

On the evening before the Day of Rage, Ghonim had dinner in Cairo with two Google employees from the US, Mathew Stepka and Jared Cohen, at an outdoor restaurant near the apartment where Ghonim was in hiding. After saying his goodbyes he walked down a dimly lit street, where three men attacked him from behind, threw him into a car, handcuffed him and took him to State Security. Afraid of being tortured, Ghonim decided to be truthful and tell his interrogators everything. "I am the founder of the page 'Kullena Khaled Said.' It was I who determined that January 25 would be the day to launch the demonstrations."

It is unlikely the police knew all this beforehand, but Ghonim apparently felt he could convince them of the righteousness of his cause or at least escape torture by telling them what they wanted to know. But from the security officers' point of view, his story was perfectly consistent with the government's version of events. This was not a "spontaneous" demonstration. Here was the administrator of the notorious Facebook page, who worked for an American company, was married to an American woman and who worked with a collaborator, Nadine Wahab, in the United States. He had just had dinner with Cohen, who only recently joined Google after a high profile job in the US State Department. Surely this was an American plot and he had dined with Cohen to receive his latest orders.

Days of Rage

On the morning of Friday the twenty-eighth, "The Day of Rage," the Egyptian government shut down all Internet and mobile phone service. It was a fatal mistake, signaling the government's weakness and that an existential crisis threatened the regime. "This is becoming the region's first telecommunications civil war," tweeted the blogger Mahmoud Salem, aka Sandmonkey. Unable to find out what was happening online, many Egyptians joined the protests to learn what was taking place in the streets.

Throughout Cairo, the mosques were filled on Friday the twenty-eighth. At a single moment tens of thousands of protesters streamed out of them, headed towards Tahrir Square. The chants of "The people want the fall of the regime" reverberated through neighborhood streets and bounced off shuttered downtown buildings; the smells of smoke and tear gas wafted in the air. Women and men, Coptic Christians and Muslims linked arms and shouted with one voice, "The people want the fall of the regime."

The world was watching on live television feeds and online video. The images of that day and the battles that followed were iconic—a lone man standing in front of a water canon; the ruling party's headquarters on fire; the crowds surging back and forth against riot police on the 6th of October Bridge over the Nile, braving volley after volley of tear gas and finally overwhelming the police; the surreal medieval combat as pro-Mubarak supporters attacked on camels; the Molotov cocktails thrown from rooftops on the mass of demonstrators in the square, protesters sitting atop tanks and a circle of Christians protecting their Muslim brothers and sisters as they knelt in prayer.

This time, having taken the Square once again, the protesters would not leave. A veritable self-governing city emerged in the heart of Cairo. Makeshift medical clinics were set up, food and water were shared among hundreds of thousands of people, and security forces were established, armed with sticks and trashcan lids to ward off the incessant attacks by government sponsored vigilantes. From his home in Washington, NPR's Andy Carvin became one of the few sources for real-time big-picture information from Tahrir Square, retweeting and reposting words and pictures that gave eyewitness accounts of what was happening as it happened. From one side of the square to another, from the national museum to the police lines, from the national library to the protesters' makeshift hospital, from lost children to reluctant army commanders, he painted a vivid picture of what became known as the Battle for Tahrir.

Carvin and others reporting via social media noted that throughout the clashes, the army's role remained ambiguous—sometimes protecting the demonstrators, sometimes allowing the pro-Mubarak forces through their ranks to attack them. In one frightening moment, two F-15 fighter jets flew low and loud over the crowd and there was concern that a Tiananmen-style massacre was about to take place. But the demonstrators embraced the army. "The people and the army are one hand," protesters shouted. Still, they were uncertain what the army would do. A statement from activist leaders demanded a formal announcement from the army generals of their position and, finally, they got it—the generals recognized the legitimate demands of the people and would protect their right to peacefully demonstrate.

On Tuesday, February 1, a "Million Man March" swelled the ranks of the protesters at Tahrir Square. Public opinion was clearly on the side of the revolution now, despite continued propaganda against it in the state media. The newly appointed vice president, Omar Suleiman, announced he would start talks with opposition parties over constitutional reforms, but the real power was in Tahrir Square.

That evening, President Mubarak addressed the nation on television and pledged he would not run for another term in the coming election, scheduled for September. In a highly emotional address Mubarak appealed to the people he had led for three decades. "I defended the soil of this homeland during peace and during war," he reminded them. "Egypt is my home. In it I was born and in it I shall die." The speech was fairly effective among the non-demonstrating viewing audience and brought a wave of sympathy for the embattled president. The crowd in Tahrir, however, watching on giant video screens, erupted in anger, demanding that the President step down immediately. Having defeated the security forces, they saw no reason to negotiate.

The next day, though, on "Bloody Wednesday," as it became known, government-paid thugs violently attacked the demonstrators while the army stood aside and would not intervene to protect them. It would be the most violent day of the revolution. Still, the protesters held their ground. Unable to suppress the uprising, the regime started attacking journalists, dozens of whom were beaten and arrested, and angry pro-Mubarak mobs began hunting foreigners.

Stuck in prison with no access to news or information, Ghonim had no idea what was happening on the street. His arrest had provoked widespread concern among his family, friends and activists. Google spared no effort in trying to locate him. Though little information emerged, the attempts to find him generated a good deal of attention from the local and international media. But then Dr. Hazem Abdel Azim—a senior government official whom Ghonim had known for some years and one of the very few people who knew Ghonim's role as the creator and Webmaster for the *Kullena Khaled Said* Facebook page—decided to reveal Ghonim's identity to the press, raising his profile as one of the key leaders of the uprising.

Mubarak's faltering regime, like those of many other authoritarian rulers, had boxed itself into a corner by eliminating any legitimate opposition. Without credible interlocutors the dictatorship had few ways to negotiate a way out of the crisis. And unlike almost all revolutionary movements that had preceded it, this was a citizens' revolution without leaders. In previous uprisings, people were organized and mobilized by a clearly defined leadership that sought to seize control of the state, replacing one elite with another. In this sense, one could argue this was, indeed, a "Facebook Revolution." Crowds, both online and on the streets, were the body and soul of the revolution. They would not be satisfied until the ruler resigned.

It is unclear how deliberately the regime sought to engage with Ghonim as a representative of the demonstrators. It was, however, the newly appointed vice president, Suleiman, who finally ordered Ghonim's release on February 6. That night, for the first time in eleven days, he was able to call his wife, who until that moment did not know whether he was still alive. It was past two in the morning in Dubai when she awoke to hear his voice. "It's me, Wael," he said excitedly. She was suspicious. "What's my mother's maiden name?" she asked. He answered and added, "She is the one that loves me more than you do," one of their private jokes. "Oh my God, Wael!" she screamed.

After some delays, Hosam Badrawy, who had just been named the new Secretary General of the ruling National Democratic Party, drove Ghonim to his mother's home. When they finally arrived there was a gaggle of reporters and cameramen who had been waiting for hours. Ghonim rushed past them, ran to the third floor and embraced his family.

Ghonim decided he should speak to the local media, though he realized he was ignorant of the events of the past eleven days. Nevertheless, he thought it would be most effective if he were to share his thoughts on his release from prison while his emotions were still raw. He called Mona el-Shazly, the host of a popular television show, and offered her an exclusive interview that very night, on two conditions. One was that he be allowed to speak freely and the other was that the channel donate a million Egyptian pounds to the families of the martyrs. Once this was agreed, he headed off with a few of his activist friends to the television studio.

The president's speech on February 1 had won the sympathy of millions of Egyptians, sparking large demonstrations calling for an end to the occupation in Tahrir Square. The regime apparently felt time was on its side, that the protests would wind down and the country would wait for elections and a peaceful transfer of power in September. Ghonim's interview was a game-changer. He began with a passionate soliloquy about the causes of the revolt and stressed that he did not want to be treated as a hero. "The real heroes of this revolution were the people who had died and been injured," he told el-Shazly. "My sacrifices could not be compared to theirs."

Exhausted from the lack of sleep, he paused at times to collect his thoughts, but remained highly emotional. When the reporter mentioned that some businessmen planned to donate money to the families of the revolution's martyrs, the victims' photos flashed on the screen behind him. Seeing the faces of so many young Egyptians "who had given their lives for a better Egypt," Ghonim was overcome by grief. He broke down, put his head in his hands and sobbed. El-Shazly begged him to stop crying, but he could only manage to say, "I would like to tell every father and mother who lost a child, I am sorry. I am sorry, but this is not our fault, it's the fault of everyone who clung on to power and would not let it go." Then he rushed out of the studio. It was at this moment that the revolution found its voice.

Once again, huge crowds took to the streets, many motivated by the interview they had seen the night before. The broadcast played endlessly on television and the Internet around the world. Ghonim's wife begged him to come home to Dubai for the sake of his family, but he felt it would betray "the many martyrs who had died for their freedom." He was tied to the revolution that his Facebook page had helped unleash.

The next day he went to Tahrir Square, which he had last seen on the twenty-fifth. It took him twenty minutes to push through the crowd to the front. In a shop behind the main stage, where speakers gathered, Khaled Said's mother entered unexpectedly and embraced him. She held him tightly and cried, saying, "My son did not die. You are my son, Khaled."

He told her that Egypt would soon be free and that Khaled's name would never be forgotten.

When he stepped to the stage Ghonim saw an ocean of people packing the immense square, and the bridges and boulevards that fed into it. Later he wrote, "Never in my life did I sense as much love in one place . . . Tahrir Square had been transformed into a utopian plot of Earth where all people could believe in their dreams . . . There really is a difference between sensing people's love online and actually experiencing it in the real world."

Over the next three days, the revolution intensified as labor strikes spread throughout the country. There was little room for compromise. The new minister of the interior and the head of State Security tried to negotiate with Ghonim at a late night meeting, but Ghonim was adamant that the president must resign. Two days later, Dr. Badrawy called Ghonim to say that he had finally convinced Mubarak to surrender power to his vice president. Badrawy asked Ghonim if he would meet Mubarak in person to present the protesters' position. Ghonim agreed.

On his way to the palace, deliriously happy, Ghonim called Maher, who had eluded arrest by sleeping in Tahrir Square, which he called "the safest place in Egypt." Ghonim invited Maher to join him "for an urgent matter." Maher agreed, but first chided, "So you fooled me, Wael. We met in Qatar only a few days before January 25 and you didn't tell me you were the '*Kullena Khaled Said*' administrator!" he mock-complained. "We'll settle this when I see you."

Instead of meeting Mubarak, however, Ghonim and Maher were intercepted by Prime Minister Shafik. It was clear he had no intention of letting them see Mubarak. As they left the prime minister's office, Ghonim apologized to Maher. On their sullen ride home, however, they were energized by a news bulletin. The international news media were reporting that Mubarak was about to resign. Their spirits soared again.

When Ghonim got home, he turned on the television news and watched President Obama congratulate the Egyptian people on achieving their goals. Jubilation spread through the streets. Raucous cheering erupted in Tahrir Square. Ghonim rushed to the square to watch Mubarak's speech from there. But as Mubarak concluded, the euphoria quickly dissipated. Instead of leaving office, he was "delegating" his authority to vice president Omar Suleiman. It was not the clear resignation the revolution demanded. A group of protesters broke away from Tahrir and began to march on the presidential palace. Ghonim returned to his Facebook page, feeling like his "computer keyboard had become a machine gun, firing bullets with every keystroke."

As Friday prayers approached, hundreds of thousands of demonstrators again flooded Tahrir Square and a large march took off for the state-broadcasting center. At about 5 p.m., television stations announced that an important statement would be issued shortly. A somber and chastened Omar Suleiman spoke the words that the protesters had shed so much blood to hear: "President Muhammad Hosni Mubarak has decided to give up the office of the president of the republic and instructed the Supreme Council of the Armed forces to manage the affairs of the country. May God guide our steps."

Revolutions are never pretty. More than eight hundred protesters died during the eighteen days it took to overthrow Mubarak. Whether Egypt achieves a true democracy or falls into sectarian intolerance will take years, perhaps decades, to determine. Having experienced freedom, however, the people of Tahrir Square will never be quite the same. The new media proved to be a transformative force in the hands of skilled and courageous activists. The challenge now will be to utilize these same tools to build a better democracy.

THE DRAGON AND
THE INTERNET

The Arab Spring would have little resonance in China. An anonymous post on China's social media sites on February 20, 2011 calling on citizens to stroll past McDonald's in the heart of the capital to launch a "Jasmine Revolution" brought out more gawkers and journalists than protesters—in addition to a vast army of security forces. Despite pervasive corruption, a yawning income gap and little rule of law or democracy, the Chinese dragon has brought wealth and power to its people to a degree not seen since the reign of Kublai Khan. In a single generation (from 1978 to 2003), China's Communist rulers reduced the number of people living below the poverty line from 250 million to just 29 million, a developmental leap unprecedented in human history. This is not fertile ground for revolution. Today, Chinese people have the right to travel, make money and, though greatly constrained, to communicate and express themselves in ways that would have been inconceivable just two decades ago.

After their humiliating defeat by the British in 1842 and (worse) by their traditional rival, the Japanese, in 1894, Chinese rulers and intellectuals realized they would have to adopt the ways of Western science and technology to defend their ancient kingdom. Under Mao Zedong, the

Communists subdued all internal opposition and solidified control over the largest nation on earth. But a series of disastrous social and economic policies left China in turmoil until Deng Xiaoping took over following Mao's death. The economic reforms he instituted in 1979 transformed China into the fastest growing economy in the world. Wary of the political reforms in Gorbachev's Russia, which Deng concluded had led to the collapse of Soviet Communism, the Chinese leader ordered a clampdown on political dissent while doubling down on economic modernization.

China's astonishing success in revamping itself from a backward peasant economy to a modern world power poses a challenge to the fundamental assumptions of Western liberalism. Can a free market succeed without democracy? Will one-party rule prove a better template for economic growth than political pluralism? Is China's model better suited for the developing world than a liberal democratic one? The country's success, especially in the context of worldwide recession and political gridlock in the United States and Europe, makes these questions particularly salient for understanding the "dictator's dilemma," when autocratic leaders are caught between their desire to participate in the global, free market economy and their fear of losing control over their people. As China embraces globalization and the information revolution, can it continue on its authoritarian path, or are these dynamics implicitly contradictory?

Vast literature exists focusing on censorship and the use of circumvention tools to avoid it and whether the Internet will be a vehicle of contention that can usher in democracy in China. We have seen how open media have undermined the legitimacy of authoritarian regimes in Russia and its satellites, Pakistan,

Georgia, Tunisia and Egypt. The Internet is undoubtedly the freest space in China today, but too great an emphasis on it as a tool for revolutionary political change misses what may be a more important point. The revolution is already happening inside China's cyberspace, whether or not it leads to imminent political change in the real world.

Despite constraints and censorship, growth in Chinese cyberspace has been exponential, transforming the social, political, and economic life of its people. Here, in a space that the blogger and Internet chronicler Hu Yong, a professor at Peking University's School of Journalism and Communications, calls the "networked civil society," cyber citizens can access alternative sources of news and information, spend their leisure time, communicate with each other, participate in non-governmental organizations, create voluntary associations, support charities, shop, date, and agitate for environmental protection, consumer rights, health, and safety. Half a billion Chinese Netizens are experiencing the first true public space in their history, a virtual training ground for democracy.

Origins of an Internet With Chinese Characteristics

Deng Xiaoping's successor, Jiang Zemin, is credited with launching China's Internet Revolution after recognizing the importance of information technologies for the building of a strong army. Creating a technologically advanced military was central to his goal of favoring growth and modernization over Mao's revolutionary ideology. The Internet, he realized, was indispensable for communications, control, and psychological motivation. His son, Dr. Jiang Mianheng, the co-founder of China Netcom, was instrumental in building the world's largest fiber-optic network in China. Jiang was confident that an Internet with "Chinese characteristics" could be controlled by the party-state and avoid the popular upheavals that followed Gorbachev's policies of glasnost.

Nationalism was the defining issue of this new space from the earliest days of the Internet. As Chinese politics coursed radically from one extreme to another—from Mao's "to rebel is justified" to Deng's "it is glorious to get rich"—nationalism remained the one constant ideological theme. This virtual public space, where citizens experienced freedom of expression for the first time, initially arose in response to anti-Chinese attacks during riots in Indonesia in May 1998 that provoked widespread anger in the new blogosphere.

After NATO bombed the Chinese Embassy in Belgrade during the war in Kosovo in May 1999, the People's Daily Online, an official publication of the party, created "Strengthening the National Forum," an online bulletin board where bloggers were encouraged to express their outrage. In "The Glory and Promise of Online Public Opinion," an article in the *Southern Weekend*, considered the most influential liberal paper in the country with the largest weekly circulation, journalists Lin Chufang and Zhao Ling argue that this first current-affairs news forum marked the emergence of the Internet as a platform for the expression of public opinion in China. Other examples of this include an April 2005 online campaign in which the Sina Corporation, the largest Chinese-language infotainment portal, collected twenty million names aimed at opposing Japan's bid for a permanent seat on the United Nations Security Council while Sohu, a rival, organized another fifteen million. Also, in 2008 a Website, www.anticnn.com, was launched to protest Western news media's coverage of riots in Tibet.

The Dragon and the Internet

But deploying the Internet to arouse nationalist fervor risks "catching the tiger by the tail." The same force of public opinion could be directed at the party-state. Indeed, over the last few years there has been a slight decrease in outward-looking nationalist campaigns as nationalism in virtual space has morphed into an inward search for national identity. There is a palpable yearning throughout Chinese society for belonging, justice, and a moral community. Given the chaotic trajectory of official Communist ideology—from the leftist rhetoric of the Cultural Revolution to the rightist triumphalism of free market capitalism—it is no wonder that Chinese citizens are eager to define a consistent national character.

The Great Firewall

In 1991, Tsinghua University set up the first Internet network on a college campus in China. Three years later, the Beijing Spectrometer, an optical device for measuring wavelengths, made the first international connection with Stanford University's Linear Accelerator Laboratory, followed by other Chinese academic institutions linking to the new World Wide Web through a dedicated line with the United States. By early 1997, ordinary citizens were allowed to connect to the Web, but the central government maintained ownership and monopoly control over all access routes. Through a series of constraints, some technical and others legal and regulatory, Chinese authorities established the "Great Firewall of China," making it difficult, if not impossible, for Chinese Internet users to access foreign Websites.

Using the most sophisticated censorship technologies now in existence, the government has corralled Internet users into its own internal Web by forcing Internet service providers to prevent specific word searches, selectively blocking international websites and, perhaps most effectively, slowing access and loading speed on Websites located on servers outside China. Given the frustrations of searching in foreign languages and the intolerably long waits and time-outs, the vast majority of Internet users in China naturally opt for the domestic providers. With the largest Internet market in the world, China has also been able to coerce multi-national technology companies like Yahoo!, Microsoft, and Cisco to go along with its censorship regime. Finally, by keeping most of its Internet users on servers located in Beijing, the government maintains the ability to track their comments and online activities after the fact, essentially curtailing free speech.

Michael Anti—one of the most popular bloggers in China who became something of an Internet rock star after Microsoft famously blocked his blog at the request of Chinese authorities in 2005—describes how "smart censorship" works in his country, a practice he calls "block and clone." At a TED Talk in July 2012 he explained, "Where you have Google, we have Baidu. You have Twitter, we have Weibo. You have Facebook, we have Renren. You have YouTube, we have Youku and Tudou. The Chinese government blocked every single international Web 2.0 service, and we Chinese copycatted every one." In this way the party-state can satisfy people's needs for social networking while maintaining control.

Weibo

Social networking sites are by far the fastest growing segment of the Chinese Web. In August 2009, following ethnic riots in Urumqi, the Chinese government shut down domestic microblogging services and blocked Twitter and Facebook. A month later, Sina launched Sina Weibo, which combined the 140-character SMS text format of Twitter with the basic functions of Facebook—private and public messaging, comments and reposts. With Sina's servers in Beijing, the authorities allow most of the benefits of social networking while maintaining ultimate control. Because 140 Chinese characters can convey far more information than 140 English letters— three and a half times as much—Weibo content is much richer than English microblogs. The introduction of Weibo unleashed an unprecedented explosion of public opinion and dialogue. In just four years, Sina Weibo attracted four hundred million users, essentially becoming a mass media in its own right with Web 2.0 characteristics.

In a sense, the Weibo phenomenon can be seen as a continuation of the Democracy Wall movement of 1978-1979 marking the end of the chaotic and self-destructive decade of the Cultural Revolution. It was in the center of Beijing, at the intersection of Xidan Road and Changan Avenue, where protesters began hanging "big character posters" on an old wall denouncing the Cultural Revolution and calling for democratic political reforms. The next decade witnessed a flowering of cultural innovation and enlightenment idealism, an innocent exuberance that followed the unprecedented free market economic reforms of Deng Xiaoping.

But this yearning for freedom came to its apotheosis and its defeat in 1989 at Tiananmen Square. Deng, afraid of catching Gorbachev's Russian flu, brought a tragic end to this movement in a hail of bullets. The violent suppression of the protests in Beijing ended what the scholar Guobin Yang calls the "epic style of the student movement" with its "grand idealism" and its naiveté. The thirst for political reform would continue, but the post-Tiananmen generation would prove to be more sophisticated and adaptive, picking its battles judiciously and employing satire and humor over confrontation.

A cat-and-mouse game exists between government censors who filter Weibo and other online content by blocking key words, and Netizens, who creatively find ways around this. But it is a game the censors inevitably will lose. In 2012, Tencent—which had introduced the first free instant messaging program called QQ, with 784 million registered active user accounts by September 2012—came out with a mobile phone voice-generated texting service called Weixin ("We Chat"). Weixin may be the game changer tilting the playing field decisively against the censors. With voice messaging, broadcast capabilities (one-to-many), photo/video applications, location sharing and other social networking features, Weixin has become an overnight national obsession. Since texting in Chinese characters involves multiple keystrokes, voice-based Weixin is far easier to use than text-based apps, increasing its popularity. Two hundred million people downloaded it within two months of its release. But most important, unlike Weibo or QQ, voice messaging cannot easily be filtered or searched for key words.

Censorship undoubtedly remains both venal and ubiquitous; but to fully understand Chinese cyberspace, it is better to compare it to what came before than to Western standards of privacy and free expression. As Hu Yong has written, "the starting point for observing China must be China." Michael Anti, whose real name is Zhao Jing, knew all too well the power of censorship in China. As a Chinese correspondent in Baghdad during the Iraq war, he lost his job when the Chinese government shut down the paper that had employed him. He turned to the less-censored Web and developed one of the largest followings of any blogger in Chinese cyberspace. Ever since Microsoft, under pressure from Beijing, shut down his blog, he has veered back and forth between a wild-eyed optimist about the democratizing role of the Internet in China to a fatalist who believes the days of free expression are over. Yet Anti, like all Chinese, experienced the exhilaration that came with even circumscribed freedom of speech. "Before, the party controlled every single piece of media, but then Chinese began logging onto discussion boards and setting up blogs, and it was as if a bell jar had lifted. Even if you were still too cautious to talk about politics, the mere idea that you could publicly state your opinion about anything—the weather, the local sports scene—felt like a bit of a revolution."

The Mother of Creativity

The majority of Internet users in China are under twenty-five, the post-Tiananmen generation. For them, the virtual world provides a place of autonomy that is not available in the real world, and the massive censorship apparatus is more of an annoyance than a limitation on their freedom. Diffuse and unorganized, the youth of China today are discovering their freedom within cyberspace, building a network civil society that is rich, independent of the state and able significantly to define the national agenda, if not yet determine state policy. A robust virtual civil society is transforming Chinese society, whether or not it ever leads to political pluralism. Compared to the restrictions that the parents of today's Netizens lived under, the network civil society offers a realm of freedom that would have been unimaginable a generation ago.

The new student activists "are more down to earth," says Professor Yang; they "are not about overthrowing state power, but rather about the defense of citizenship rights, the violations of pre-existing entitlements, and the building of new forms of civic association . . . Political transformation may well begin with a new cultural revolution, and online activism represents nothing less."

The government's efforts to control news and opinion by blocking key search words is often met more with mockery than fear or anger by young Netizens. "Censorship warps us in many ways, but it is also the mother of creativity," says Hu Yong. Using parody to poke fun at and circumvent censorship has become something of a national pastime. The Chinese word *egao*, borrowed originally from the Japanese word *kuso*, or "shit," refers to this ridiculing of the language authorities use through a variety of textual and video reconstructions. A classic example is a play on the word "harmony," after Chinese president Hu Jintao proposed the slogan "to build a harmonious socialist society" as his signature theme. Internet users appropriated the word as a substitute for censorship, turning it into a verb, such as, "My blog was harmonized."

The word "river crab" is pronounced the same as "harmony;" so after that word became forbidden to use in online forums, browsers substituted "river crab" instead. In a similar way, a "grass mud horse" is a homonym for "motherfucker." It was originally used by online video game players of *World of Warcraft* to avoid restrictions on expressions of vulgarity, but was soon adopted more widely to mock all forms of censorship. When the government launched an "anti-vulgarity" campaign in January 2009 that shut down 1,900 political websites and 250 blogs, cyber activists began circulating tales of a mythical conflict between the grass mud horse and the river crab that generated millions of hits and spawned a virtual industry of art works, music videos and even stuffed animals.

Such mockery can take on a more subversive tone when coupled with online protests. After a high-speed train crash killed forty people in Wenzhou on July 23, 2011, bloggers expressed outrage that the authorities had quickly buried a damaged railcar in a literal cover up and later found an unconscious two-year-old girl in the remaining wreckage, long after officials had given up searching for survivors. In one online poll after the accident, 98 percent of respondents believed railway officials had undertaken these actions to destroy evidence. The Party's Department of Propaganda responded by issuing orders to all media to block any articles about high-speed trains: "Do not publicize people's reflections." At a press conference a few days after the accident, Wang Yongping, a spokesman for the Ministry of Railways, was asked how workers had found the toddler alive. He responded, "I can only say that this was a miracle! Anyway, I believe it!" Soon his words reverberated through Chinese cyberspace and became a derisive phrase that entered into everyday conversation. "There is no traffic jam in Beijing today," went one version. "This is a miracle. Whether you believe it or not, I believe it anyway."

But *egao* is not confined to textual satire; more and more of it appears on films and in video blogs and animation. The word first entered the popular lexicon in 2006 when a $30 million movie called *The Promise*, heavily promoted as an extraordinary work of art, was widely panned. An audio engineer in Shanghai, Hu Ge, reconstructed scenes from the original into a farcical critique of current events along the lines of a popular crime show. Hu's film, *A Bloody Case Caused by A Steamed Bun* went viral, attracting tens of millions of viewers and sparking a host of online video spoofs.

One of the best-known *egao* artists is Pi San, an online animator who first rose to prominence with a provocative cartoon character named Kuang Kuang. In 2009, a Kuang Kuang video called *Blow Up The School* became an instant Internet sensation among Chinese youth, turning the bubble-headed character into a minor cult figure. Pi San has enjoyed his fame, but tries to steer clear of the Internet censors. In January 2011, he came close to crossing the line with *Little Rabbit, Be Good*, a four-minute video greeting card to mark the Year of the Rabbit. What begins as a soothing bedtime fairy tale about bunny rabbits turns into a nightmare depicting some of the most egregious scandals that have rocked the establishment. Tigers rule the "harmonious forest" where babies die from poisoned milk, a protester fighting forced evictions is crushed under a tiger's car, a hit-and-run driver kills a rabbit and boasts of his high-level police connections—allegories of real-life events that had provoked tens of millions to protest online. In the end, the rabbits rise up in revolt and devour the tigers. By the time censors began deleting copies from the nation's Websites, four million people had watched the video.

It is often difficult for activists or artists to know how the government censors will react. David Bandurski, the online editor of the China Media Project at Hong Kong University, argues, "The government's primary means of control is a fuzzy line. No one ever knows exactly where the line is. The control apparatus is built on uncertainty and self-censorship, on creating this atmosphere of fear."

Crossing the Line

More sophisticated Netizens continue to use proxy servers and other circumvention tools to access Western websites like YouTube and Twitter. Even though it is blocked throughout China, Twitter continues to have tens of thousands of active users who have developed an informal open Internet advocacy network. However, because it is cumbersome to access Twitter through overseas proxy servers, it remains a relatively marginal force in China, far eclipsed by domestic competitors.

Nevertheless, when the blogger Guo Baofeng was arrested for reposting a video in which the mother of a gang-raped murder victim accused police in Xiamen of a cover-up, he managed to send out a Tweet to his friends. Adapting a popular phrase that had been circulating in the massive gaming community, Wen Yunchao, one of Guo's blogger friends, called on his followers to send postcards to the police station where Guo was being held, on which they wrote: "Guo Baofeng, your mother wants you to go home to eat." Inundated with these postcards, the police backed down and released him after sixteen days in prison.

Wen's story is instructive. Reared in poverty in rural Guangdong Province, he had supported the army's crackdown on the pro-democracy protesters in Tiananmen Square while still a student. But one evening after ending his shift at a power station near Guangzhou, Wen watched a television documentary aired in nearby Hong Kong about the 1989 massacre that contradicted the official narrative. An Internet search confirmed what was contained in the film. Over the next decade he became a voracious researcher and built a large following for his blog, Ramblings of a Drunkard, published under the pen name Bei Feng.

Like all dissident bloggers, Bei Feng never knew what might land him in trouble. In 2009, on the anniversary of the death of Mao Zedong, he started a "de-Maoification" campaign online. Realizing that the authorities could not trawl through photographs like they could for censored words, Bei Feng used images instead of text. "Mao" is also the word for "hair," so he urged his Twitter and Weibo followers to post pictures of before-and-after shots of shaved body parts, literally "getting rid of mao." Such irreverence about the founding icon of the party-state would seem dangerous, but no reprisals followed.

When the government arrested Nobel laureate Liu Xiaobo, preventing him from receiving his award in Oslo, they also blocked phrases like "empty chair" from the Internet that browsers might use to circumvent the censors. So, Bei Feng decided to post pictures of empty chairs. "If we only watch," he implored his followers, "then one day [the empty chair] might appear by your family's dining table as well."

But three months later, while visiting Hong Kong just after the Arab Spring revolutions spooked China's leaders, Bei Feng received an email warning from Chinese security agents: "Don't come home. You'll be arrested before you even see your wife and son." He remained in Hong Kong for three years until he was forced into exile in the United States at the end of 2012.

A Crisis of Legitimacy

The widespread use of parody in China's cyberspace would seem to indicate a wholesale lack of trust in the party-state. As George Orwell once said, "Every joke is a tiny revolution."

Many believe the Communist Party suffers from a legitimacy crisis that is undermining its authority and might someday threaten its rule. In a Confucian culture that emphasizes the veneration of authority, mockery suggests a lack of respect. Sociologists and political scientists debate the extent or even the existence of such a crisis. But clearly this is an issue keeping leaders of the party up at night. In the absence of any legal political opposition, a lack of trust in the party is tantamount to a lack of trust in the state itself. There is no alternative party that can be judged to be relatively more or less trustworthy. The underlying rationale for the legitimacy of the party-state is reduced to "us or chaos," a refrain repeated by every dictatorship. Without an ability to vote for a different party, revolution remains the only alternative.

In lieu of any political opposition, party leaders in Beijing are more apt to ward off popular protests by blaming local officials. Studies of Chinese people's trust in government show a sharp decline from the center to the local—the exact inverse of the democratic paradigm, where voters tend to trust their local representatives more than their national leaders. In a poll of rural Chinese citizens, trust in the government declined from 50 percent for the central authorities to 1 percent for local governors. In China, there has been a long tradition of a belief in the goodness of the Emperor and a corresponding belief that those around him are corrupt. Political power in China runs in a vertical axis from the local to the center. Top party officials have become skillful in deflecting criticism away from Beijing to local leaders. The center's control of most Internet servers has become a potent tool in their strategy. When bloggers criticize local authorities, the local government doesn't have access to the data in Beijing. By not censoring certain online criticism, party officials in Beijing can punish or control local cadres. It is, therefore, not surprising that virtually all major online protests have been directed at local officials.

But allowing or even encouraging massive online criticisms of local leaders, "Weibo justice," as it is known, cedes a degree of political power to citizens outside of party control. Under Mao it was the Supreme Leader who initiated and defined political campaigns for the masses, but today popular pressure is often generated from the grass roots, and party leaders are forced to respond by either suppressing dissent or redirecting it against their political rivals.

Weibo has now become China's Fourth Estate. Isaac Mao, one of China's first bloggers, points out, "Before the emergence of Weibo, local people actually had limited channels to try and solve their problems. Weibo is a kind of pressure politics on local government officials." When millions of citizens in a one-party state express their revulsion at injustice, the government has little choice but to act. As the exclusive authority, the party-state is held accountable for everything that takes place in the realm. Paradoxically, in a multi-party democracy, the majority party has more leeway to ignore popular opposition while courts are tasked with resolving most moral injustices. But in China, the party becomes the sole arbiter of all disputes and is ultimately responsible.

Before Weibo, local authorities could act with impunity. In 2006, Tang Hui's eleven-year-old daughter was kidnapped and forced into prostitution in a brothel in the central Chinese city of Yongzhou. After receiving a tip about her daughter's location, Tang called the police, but they refused to arrest anyone. "They said this was not a criminal case," she recounted. For six years, Tang campaigned tirelessly for justice. Eventually, a court convicted the brothel owner, but Tang continued to demand public punishment for the police who had shielded him all along. Summoned to police headquarters, Tang was arrested and ordered imprisoned in a reeducation labor camp for eighteen months without a trial. When her lawyer posted an account of her ordeal on Weibo, it quickly went viral. Thirty million Weibo users commented, turning the issue into national news. Within ten days of her incarceration, China Central Television announced Tang's release.

Virtual Public Space and the Emergence of the Network Civil Society

By 2007, public opinion on the Internet had come into its own. In June of that year a group of fathers published an open letter on the Tianya Club forum, one of the most popular spaces where Netizens could express their opinions on a wide range of topics. The fathers told a harrowing tale of travelling from their homes in Henan Province to Shanxi Province to rescue their children from a kidnapping racket that forced them to work as slaves shoveling coal into brick kilns. The fathers rescued about forty of the kids, but another two thousand, they claimed, were still enslaved. The response on the Internet was ferocious.

Photos of missing children began circulating and investigations soon revealed that police and local party officials were profiting from the kidnapping and slavery business. State propaganda authorities ordered all online forums, blogs, and Websites to close the comment function in any related news reports. *China Digital Times* published an internal directive it had obtained from the State Council Information Office, which said: "Harmful information that uses this event to attack the party and the government should be deleted as soon as possible." But the cacophony on the Web forced General Secretary Hú Jintao and Prime Minister Wen Jiabao to express their concerns. While it sought to keep online public opinion under control, the central government also dispatched thirty-five thousand police officers to raid seventy-five hundred kiln operations and brought charges against ninety-five local officials.

From Virtual to Real

Weibo justice gives the network civil society a certain measure of supervisory influence over the otherwise unlimited power of local authorities, but leading party officials never countenance any online activities that are used to organize offline protests. Apparently they were caught off-guard when ten thousand followers of the Falun Gong religious sect demonstrated against the state on April 25, 1999 outside Zhongnanhai, the palace adjacent to the Forbidden City that is the command center of the party and government. Organized covertly by email like a flash mob, the protest frightened President Jiang Zemin, who ordered a crackdown on the organization. Ever since the Zhongnanhai event, any online commentary that calls for real world protests, particularly at the national level, provokes a massive and disproportionate response from the government. Nevertheless, the number of "mass incidents" continues to rise each year, largely in rural areas, but the government prevents these disparate groups from coordinating their protests with similar-minded compatriots.

Ironically, the party's greatest fear is that the country's

workers will organize against a state that was built on "proletarian solidarity." Tens of millions of young men and women who have migrated in search of work from rural areas in the center of the country to the vast industrial cities along the east coast suffer from abominable working conditions and low wages. Usually, they are separated from their families, the traditional bedrock of Chinese society.

One such migrant worker is Tan Guocheng, who grew up among the rice paddies and orange groves in a small farming community near the city of Shaoyang, in central China's Hunan Province, where Mao Zedong was born. His family's small plot of land was not enough to support him, his brother, and sister, so the siblings left for factory jobs in the east. Four years later, in 2010, the twenty-two-year-old Tan was engaged to a fellow worker, but his $175 monthly salary at a Honda transmission factory in Foshan was not enough to buy a house or raise a family. Workers there were growing increasingly angry after Honda management offered them a meager $7-a-month raise. Labor tensions were generally on the rise that year, highlighted by the suicides of fourteen workers at Foxconn plants. On May 17, Tan pressed an emergency button shutting down his production line and walked out with a hundred workers. After he and a fellow strike leader were arrested, the entire factory went on strike. Despite beatings and threats, they held out and won 35 percent raises.

The Foshan strikes were originally covered in the state-run media, but as workers at other Honda plants began sharing news online, the government banned further commentary. Like many other migrant workers, those at a Honda Lock auto parts factory in Zhongshan, fourteen miles from Foshan, are tech savvy, part of China's first generation of digital natives. They set up Internet forums, communicated with the strikers in Foshan and furtively uploaded videos of Honda Lock security guards beating up employees. Using QQ, the popular instant-messaging service, they began organizing for a strike of their own. But they soon learned that QQ offered no protection from eavesdropping and surveillance, so they switched to more secure mobile applications. Days after the Foshan strike ended, the seventeen hundred workers at Honda Lock went out on strike. The results of the Zhongshan walkout were mixed; nonetheless, the fact that the strikers were able to organize online demonstrated the potential for digital tools to accelerate offline strife. The relative freedom of expression in Chinese cyberspace, unique in China's otherwise closed society, opens new space for real world contention.

While party officials appear most threatened by any unsanctioned online organizing by workers or religious sects like the Falun Gong, they have been surprisingly tolerant of digital activism regarding the environment. An independent, non-governmental environmental movement was born in Yunnan Province in 1995 when Long Yongcheng, an intrepid ecologist, led a group of local farmers to block logging trucks in order to protect the last remaining refuge for golden monkeys. Thought for decades to be extinct, this creature had never been photographed until Long managed to do so. The sitin and the resulting preservation of the monkeys' old growth habitat in the Laojun Mountains caught the imagination of the country.

Two years later, a colleague of Long's, Wang Yongcheng, invited a group of environmental activists and journalists to her home for what became a monthly salon, launching a countrywide environmental movement. Wang produced a weekly program about environmental protection on China

National Radio that attracted one of the largest radio audiences in China. In 1997, she formed Green Earth Volunteers, a grassroots non-governmental organization, and led a campaign to stop the damming of the Nu River.

The green movement in China has remained largely virtual and non-contentious despite the alarming state of China's environment, but more and more communities are taking to the streets to protect their health and the local environment. In one of the first of these protests, in 2007, thousands of people marched in Xiamen, a picturesque seaport in southern China, to demand the relocation of a billion-dollar petrochemical plant. The protests against the production of a highly toxic chemical—paraxylene (PX), used to make plastics and polyesters—took off after an exposé of the hazards of PX circulated on the Internet. Local authorities tried to block the blog that had posted the article but weren't able to, as the servers were in Beijing. The protests continued, attracting coverage in more liberal media outlets and in the international press and, after two public hearings, the plant was relocated. This rare offline victory was hailed as a turning point that showed the power of the Internet. The more outspoken *Southern People's Weekly* elected "Xiamen citizens" as its "people of the year"; even the official Xinhua News Agency praised the outcome as indicating a "change in the weight given to the views of ordinary Chinese in recent years."

Serve the People

Labor strife, environmental protests and political mockery are important elements of the network civil society in China, but what is most conspicuous are the millions of online communities. There seems to be an insatiable desire for community—an understandable reaction to the country's one-child policy, the movement of large numbers of people away from their ancestral roots, as well as other social displacements associated with the introduction of a market economy. Organizations independent of Communist Party rule simply didn't exist prior to the Internet.

"What is most striking about Chinese online communities," noted Guobin Yang, "is how they nurture moral sentiments." Charity and volunteerism are at the heart of the online community. By the end of 2010, there were 445,000 registered non-profit organizations and over 31 million volunteers, from providers of free school lunches to groups searching for missing children, that comprise what the scholars Shaoguang Wang and He Jianyu call an "associational revolution." These online communities do not challenge the legitimacy of the state, but they do represent an entirely unprecedented degree of autonomy from the state.

The growth of online communities has made it increasingly difficult for the government to completely control its information space. In November 2002, the first two cases of Severe Acute Respiratory Symptoms (SARS), were discovered in Guangdong, the most populous province in the country, located on the South China Sea. Local officials in Guangdong suppressed information about the disease, partly out of fear that it might affect foreign investment and partly for political reasons, as the outbreak came just after the Sixteenth Chinese Communist Party's National Congress had chosen new leadership for the province. Saving face in China can sometimes be more important than saving lives.

Despite the efforts at information control, news of the

deadly flulike virus circulated in Chinese cyberspace, catching the attention of the Global Public Health Intelligence Network that trawls the web for hints of new infectious disease epidemics. But the information quarantine didn't end until April 8, 2003, when Jiang Yanyong, the chief physician at the 301 Military Hospital in Beijing, bravely told Susan Jakes of *Time* magazine about the cover-up. (A year later, when Dr. Jiang wrote an open letter to Premier Wen Jiabao asking for a re-examination of the Tiananmen Square massacre, he and his wife were arrested and placed under military custody.)

Chinese government leaders were embarrassed at the international uproar following the *Time* exposé and they worried news leaks and rumors might spawn widespread panic. They criticized provincial leaders and fired the minister of health, Zhang Wenkang, and the mayor of Beijing, Meng Xuenon. Both were blamed for withholding information about the disease. Official news media then began covering the epidemic. The Internet, which had already offered a means to circumvent the previous news blackout, now proved indispensable in dealing with the spreading crisis. The government turned to online associations to mobilize volunteers, provide public health information to supplement its woefully inadequate rural health care system, and prevent stigma and rumors.

If the SARS epidemic showed the futility of information suppression in responding to a national crisis, the Sichuan earthquake of May 2008 proved the power of open media for national catharsis. Measuring 7.9 on the Richter scale, the quake killed 69,000 people and left 4.8 million homeless. The government response was immediate and effective, earning it near-universal praise.

It was Twitter, though, that first published reports of the

earthquake and, with the temporary relaxation of political control, Weibo and other social media platforms provided a primary source of news and emotional release. Even with saturation coverage on central television, more people followed news of the disaster on the Internet.

With uncharacteristic national solidarity, citizens and non-governmental organizations mobilized alongside the government in an extraordinary display of the power of the new civil society. Unlike previous crises, the government demonstrated remarkable candor in this case, providing round-the-clock coverage in state-run media. Photos and video news reports showed the extent of the damage, with scenes of relief workers, heroic survivors and the tragic tales of victims. Much of the civic engagement came from Websites, blogs, mailing lists, bulletin boards, and various social networks. Civic groups coordinated their activities openly, helping to raise money, direct volunteer relief efforts, and solicit blood donations.

In the weeks after the popular approval of the government's handling of the disaster and its initial media openness, a corruption scandal coursed through the Internet and rekindled dissent. Seven thousand schools had collapsed in the earthquake, killing upwards of ten thousand children. Citizen journalists uncovered evidence of shoddy construction and accused local government officials and contractors of taking shortcuts and siphoning off funds earmarked for building materials, leading to the devastation. Photos of older schools that suffered little damage and of buildings left intact adjacent to the rubble of schools fed passions over the scandal.

With the Beijing Olympics about to begin, authorities moved forcefully to choke off dissent. Parents of the dead children were offered up to $20,000, if they agreed to keep quiet.

The renowned artist Ai Weiwei, whose most controversial art project involved an exhibition of school backpacks meant to represent the thousands of kids who were killed, was beaten by security forces as he traveled to Chengdu, the provincial capital of Sichuan, to investigate the school collapses and support the parents. Bloggers were arrested and the news media were ordered to stop reporting on the tragedy.

A Harmonious Society?

The mixture of responses that followed the Sichuan earthquake—government and citizens alike banding together to assist the survivors, the government's quashing of criticism following the schoolhouse scandal—is typical of Chinese society. Whatever one can say about China seems also to be true of its opposite. Observers of China invariably are forced to declare "on the one hand this, on the other hand that." The paradoxical nature of the culture makes any predictions about its future futile.

There are many scholars and activists who proclaim the Internet poses such a contradiction to the authoritarian regime that it will inevitably lead to its overthrow. They seem to believe that if censorship were removed, the Chinese people would rush into the arms of democracy. Others think the mechanisms of control inside the Great Firewall are so strong as to preclude any challenge to the political monopoly of the party-state. Such simplistic ideas ignore the realities of Chinese society, which is both complex and ever changing.

Since the victory of the Chinese Communists in 1948, the nation has swung from the delusional utopian idealism of the Great Leap Forward to the paranoid self-destructive catharsis of the Cultural Revolution, only to adopt a pragmatic, non-ideological businessfriendly mercantilism. In the memory of those still alive, China has grown from one of the poorest nations on earth to the cusp of becoming the richest. Great pride in the country's cultural history mixes with the meme of national humiliation at the hands of foreign invaders. In *China: The Pessoptimist Nation*, William A. Callahan writes, "China's national aesthetic entails the combination of a superiority complex, and an inferiority complex." The "harmonious society" that China seeks to be is tempered by the actuality of unbridled and often contradictory economic, cultural, and political forces that compete for dominance.

The Chinese Communist Party, like all authoritarian rulers, bases its legitimacy on its stewardship of the economy and its ability to protect the nation from outside threats and internal chaos. An ancient Chinese proverb says, "There cannot be two dragons in the same pond;" but the absence of any organized and institutionalized opposition to one-party rule—like independent trade unions, churches or political parties—puts the Communists in a box. In order to maintain its legitimacy, the party-state must continuously grow the economy and maintain social order. Traditional Confucian ethics, while respecting hierarchy, harmony, and devotion to the family and state, also decree that rulers can lose "the mantle of heaven" if they fail to provide for the common good. With no alternative institutions, the party is prone to be a victim of rising expectations.

The Internet and digital communications technologies sit at the center of this maelstrom. The state has ceded considerable ground to the network civil society, but almost no political authority. Some, like imprisoned Nobel Peace Prize laureate Liu Xiaobo, believe that a growing awareness of the rights of citizens and their sense of justice pose a real threat to "the thinness of the superficial stability under authoritarian power." Whatever the future holds, however, it is undeniably true that cyberspace is where Chinese citizens experience the greatest freedom. They may not have political power, but they do have a voice. And therein may lie China's future.

CONCLUSION

As previous chapters have demonstrated, media have increasingly become a driving force in human development—not only a Fourth Estate reporting on the activities of the government and society, but a dynamic and determinative force that shapes our politics, economics, culture, and history.

The information revolution increasingly puts the destiny of humanity in our own hands. Just as our political evolution has progressively moved us from control by the few to the many, so too does the democratization of media give each of us access to information and a voice. Free, open and independent media are the means by which citizens can hold their governments accountable. Amartya Sen's insight, noted in the introduction, that no famine has ever occurred where there are free elections and a free press, gets to the heart of the matter. It is only by controlling and curtailing information that despots can rule.

The shift from information darkness to the richness of the interconnected World Wide Web provides an opportunity for all of us to determine our destiny. Heretofore, we have been the objects of forces and events that have largely been outside our control. Only a few generations ago, we discovered the scientific method, which gave us the ability to explain the world and, consequently, to learn from our mistakes. There is still some question whether ideological fundamentalism and old fashioned bad habits will win out and cause our ultimate demise; but there's a fair chance that in the generations to come, people—connected and illuminated by media—may yet find their way to a place of sustainable development.

That time might be upon us. It is hard to believe our world can simultaneously support the invention of the iPhone and acts of grotesque, indiscriminant terrorism against civilians; that we can create life in a test tube, travel to Mars, develop quantum computers and still allow millions to die from hunger.

Journalism, perhaps as much as education, will be vital to our progress. Indeed, the roles of journalists and educators will increasingly grow closer. Journalism, like science, is based on objectivity and impartiality. Given the inherently public nature of their output, journalists have a social responsibility as well as a professional one. What constitutes the news is a question that frames the human agenda. Whether we allow the news to succumb to our basest instincts, indulging ourselves in trivia and sensationalism, or restore the news to its higher public interest function is a question of great import.

There are several trends we can anticipate as journalism finds its place in the emerging information economy. Increasingly, citizen journalists will tell news in real time. And no matter what technological innovations appear, radio will continue to be a primary source of information for vast parts of the developing world for years to come. As the cost of producing and distributing news content continues to fall—the phone in my pocket can do what it took a television studio and a network to produce just a decade ago—and smart phones become ubiquitous, virtually anyone can become a journalist and a broadcaster. Professional journalists will bemoan the loss of their craft, as all craftsmen have done throughout history, and media owners will lament the loss of their profits.

But the disintermediation of the news will ultimately benefit society, as consumers of information become its producers, responsible for the story.

The exponential growth of public data, from government statistics to published research, will create an industry of data journalists able to mine, aggregate, analyze, interpret, and publicize its meaning. This information wealth will fuel economic growth. Good data is essential to well-functioning markets. A year-long study by Internews and the World Bank Institute in 2012, funded by the Gates Foundation, found a direct, sometimes causative, relationship between the degree of open media and economic growth. Indeed, the collapse of the housing market in America that precipitated the world economic recession of 2008 can largely be blamed on poor data, as the renowned Peruvian economist Hernando de Soto has shown. Data journalism will transform everything—from government, finance, and public policy to scientific and medical research, education, health, and the environment.

Finally, we are seeing the beginning of the end of all but the most coercive dictatorships. Despots control their societies largely through fear and the manipulation of information. But even in the least democratic countries, leaders depend on some minimal consensus of legitimacy. Free and independent media are anathema to their rule. As information increasingly gets into the hands of everyone, the yearning to speak freely and participate in society can only grow. What we do with this freedom is up to us.

ACKNOWLEDGEMENTS

Writing a book is an intensely personal experience, a meditation, but one that is also totally dependent on others. I could not have persevered without the unconditional love and daily support of my lover, wife, and partner Jane Rogers. A former journalist, she also proved to be a superb editor. My gratitude for her help cannot adequately be expressed in words.

The idea for this book came from my Internews board chair, Simone Coxe, who understood the benefit of pushing me out of my comfort zone. Jillian Manus, with her uncanny vision, took the germ of an idea and turned it into something much grander in scope. But moving from an idea to implementation required the extraordinary skills and patience of three very talented editors. Working with Joan Hamilton on the first half of the book was a writer's workshop for one, an extraordinary gift for which I will always be grateful. Mindy Werner picked up where Joan left off and was a superb mentor. And Jane, bravely, oversaw everything with love and tough love and more than once picked me up off the floor. At the end of the day, after all is said and done, a manuscript turns into a book through the loving care of one's agent and publisher. I had the good fortune of having as my agent George

Greenfield at Creative Well who saw the vision and jumped in with all his heart and soul. Anthony Garrett, my partner and brother, an indomitable force of nature—the person you want in your foxhole who hates more than anything to lose a battle, and rarely does—was behind me every step of the way. Stephen Shepard, the founding dean of the CUNY Graduate School of Journalism and a legend in American journalism, who started the CUNY Journalism Press, believed in the book, which was the ultimate validation for me. CUNY's skilled editor, Tim Harper, has been greatly supportive and a true pleasure to work with.

The book was only possible because of the generous support of Internews. First and foremost I must thank Jeanne Bourgault, who took over from me as president and CEO. For the last thirty-two years, Internews has been at the center of my life. I feel blessed to be able to turn over the leadership of this organization I so love and admire to someone whose executive skills far surpass my own. I am grateful to the current board members of Internews, who have supported me in innumerable ways during the writing of this book: Chris Boskin, Douglas Carlston, Matt Chanoff, Simone Coxe, Lorne Craner, Monique Maddy, Jillian Manus, Maureen Orth, James Rosenfield Sr., Cristiana Falcone Sorrell, Sandy Socolow, and John Walsh.

NGOs like Internews exist only because of the generous support of their funders. Wade Greene, Jerry Hirsch, and Simone Coxe each contributed to this book and have been among the most generous funders of this work for many years. I am grateful to count them among my closest friends.

I have had the exceptional good fortune of knowing many of the people whose courageous acts I try to describe in these pages. Kim Spencer and Evelyn Messinger, my partners in starting Internews, are the unsung heroes of citizen diplomacy, media revolutionaries who pioneered the use of new communications technologies for peace and democracy. Johnny West, the T.E. Lawrence of media, is the most creative thinker I have ever known, with that rarest of abilities to turn his ideas into action. Manana Aslamazyan has rightly been called the "mother of media development." Now in exile from Russia, she, more than anyone, paved the way for the growth of hundreds of media development NGOs around the world. We all owe her a debt of gratitude. Eduard Sagalaev and Vladimir Pozner, whom I had the privilege to know during the transformational years when the Soviet Union dissolved, played pivotal roles in opening up that closed society and ultimately preventing its violent demise. Erosi Kitsmarishvili is a master at giving other people credit for his historic accomplishments. It's a special pleasure, therefore, to be able to acknowledge him for his unique leadership role in Georgia's "Rose Revolution" and for the generous time he gave me in the writing of this book. Mir Ibrahim Rahman is a great friend and the most thoughtful, open-minded, and strategic young leader I have ever met. If Pakistan survives as a tolerant and democratic nation, it will largely be thanks to him. I will forever be indebted to his father, Mir Shakil ur Rahman, for introducing his son to me. In Burma, U Thiha Saw, Ahr Mahn, and Nyein Nyein Naing are bravely putting independent media at the forefront of the improbable democratic transformation happening in their country. Their fearlessness is an inspiration. I've only met Veran Matic once, when we testified before a Senate Committee; but it was easy to grasp the strength of character of this man who consistently stood up to the brutal dictatorship of Milosevic's Yugoslavia. One of the added benefits of writing this book has been getting to know H. E. Bitange Ndemo, the permanent secretary for information, in Kenya. A man on a mission, Ndemo is a true revolutionary whose vision is infectious and irresistible. Kathleen Reen, Mark Frohardt, and Jacobo Quintanilla are colleagues and longtime friends. Their passion and commitment to bringing information to those most in need of it and their lifelong pursuit of freedom is what keeps me in this field.

I owe great debts of gratitude to many friends and colleagues who've helped me understand the subject matter, wrote books or articles on which I relied, supported this research, fact checked everything and otherwise contributed to the writing of the book. First and foremost is Susan Clay Rosso, my assistant, whose perfection and professionalism constantly kept me from falling on my face. Joan and Bill Briggs provided a writer's paradise. Bob Fuller, as always, is my intellectual mentor. Kathy Bushkin Calvin remains my best friend and greatest supporter.

Writing about media and the fall of the Soviet Union would simply be impossible without the definitive work of Ellen Mickiewicz. Natasha Novikova helped with the research. Cheryl Mendonsa was my co-conspirator in creating the *Capital to Capital* series, with much help from the late Peter Jennings, Roone Arledge, David Burke, and, most especially, the late Congressman George E. Brown, Jr. The chapter on Afghanistan depended on the generous help of John Langlois, George Papagiannis, Sanjar Qiam, Jan McArthur, Charmaine Anderson, Ahmed Rashid, Mir Abdul Wahed Hashimi, Masood Farivar, and Ken Auletta's excellent profile of Tolo TV for *The New Yorker*.

The story of the media's role in the overthrow of President Musharraf in the chapter "The Dictator's Dilemma" was largely informed by conversations and correspondence with

Adnan Rehmat, Najam Sethi, Jugnu Mohsin, Ahmed Rashid, Oren Murphy, Mir Ibrahim Rahman, and Arnold Wafula. Besides a long interview with Erosi Kitsmarishvili, I learned the background of the "Rose Revolution" in Georgia from my colleague David Anable's excellent book on the revolt.

In Burma, I had the good fortune of interviewing Alison Campbell, U Thiha Saw, Lyndal Barry, Nyein Nyein Naing, Ahr Mahn, and Ko Sai, and relied on Christina Fink's seminal books.

To try to make sense of the complicated history of Yugoslavia and Rwanda, I relied extensively on writings or interviews with friends and colleagues like Sasa Vucinic, Wanda Hall, Sue Folger, Slava Djukic, Haris Pasovic, Laura Silber and Allan Little, Samantha Power, Allan Thompson, and Vanessa Vasic-Janekovic.

In Kenya, besides my extensive interviews with Bitange Ndemo, I had the generous help of Deborah Ensor, Ida Jooste, Brice Rambaud, Washington Onyango Akumu, Chris Finch, George Muiruri, Eric Hersman Chris Muthama, and John Marks.

The chapter "After the Deluge" relied on long interviews with the principals and superb fact checking by Anahi Ayala and Neil Scott.

Jamal Dajani, Ivan Sigal, Courtney Radsch, David Faris, Ed Bice, Anas Qtiesh, Paul Eedle, Daniel Kaufmann, and Mohamed Nanabhay helped me understand the story of Tunisia and the Arab Spring. Likewise, Andrea Bosch, Jamal Dajani, Ahmed Lutfy, Esraa Abdel Fattah, Ismail Alexandrani, Amira Maaty, and my good friend Mohamed Gohar contributed to the chapter on Egypt's Tahrir Square revolution.

The most satisfying chapter for me to write may have been

the final one on China because I learned so much trying to grasp the enigma that is Chinese cyberspace. Helping me to unravel this puzzle have been some of the most delightful people I have had the honor to work with: Filip Noubel, Xiao Quiang, Guobin Yang, Guo Liang, Yong Hu, Yuanxi Huang, Rebecca MacKinnon, Louis Berney, and Brook Larmer.

Others who have consistently supported this work include David Michaelis, Tara Sonenshine, Peter Pennekamp, Susan Rice, Pat Mitchell, Greg Carr, Larry Irving, Ellen Hume, Raisa Scriabine, Carlos Pascual, Markos Kounalakis, Loraine Safly, Hon. James A. Leach, Hon. Lee Hamilton, George Soros, Aryeh Neier, Bob Boorstin, Monroe Price, Carl Gershman, Marguerite Sullivan, Kim Spencer, Evelyn Messinger, John Hamilton Fish, David Creekmore, Laura Stein Lindamood, Annette Makino, Leslie Cushman, Pat Chadwick, Larry Kuhn, Oliver Blum, Carolyn Powers, Marjorie Rouse, Teri Carhart, Bridget Gallagher, David Rosen, Erica Feldkamp, James Fahn, Nguyen Hue, Mark Harvey, Jeanne Girardot, Bettina Peters, Aidan White and Sophie Boudry.

If I inadvertently left someone out, please accept this author's sincere apology. Thank you to all. I am deeply grateful. I have been so blessed to know such people.

ABOUT THE AUTHOR

David Hoffman is president emeritus and founder of Internews, a global non-profit organization that fosters independent media and access to information worldwide. The organization has helped build thousands of television and radio stations in some of the most difficult environments in the world that reach hundreds of millions of people.

Hoffman has written widely about media and democracy, the Internet, and the importance of supporting pluralistic, local media around the world. His articles and op-eds have appeared in *The New York Times, Foreign Affairs, The Washington Post, The Wall Street Journal, The International Herald Tribune,* and *The San Francisco Chronicle.* He has also testified before US House and Senate committees on issues of press freedom and access to information.

Hoffman was project director of the internationally acclaimed and Emmy-award winning television series *Capital to Capital* (1987-1990), produced in association with ABC News and Soviet State Television; he organized broadcasts of the War Crimes Tribunal for the former Yugoslavia and Rwanda, for which Internews was awarded the first European Commission's ECHO Award in 1996.

Hoffman was a founder of and serves as chairman emeritus of the Global Forum for Media Development, a cross-sector initiative of more than 500 leading media assistance organizations from over 100 countries. From 1980-1982, he was the editor of *Evolutionary Blues,* a journal of political thought on international conflict, the threat of nuclear war, and US-Soviet relations. Prior to that, he was national director of Survival Summer, the coalition of 140 national peace and environmental organizations that launched the peace movement of the 1980s.

Hoffman has a BA in political science from Johns Hopkins University and has completed doctoral work at the University of Colorado on the social and intellectual history of the United States.